October 5, 2019

Lori:

I created this to
heal + help others.
I Hope this Brightens
Your light.
Keep shining!

Namaste

Hello
My Name Is
Santa

An alcoholic's journey from
homelessness to Santa Claus

Brill, age 12, playing little league baseball (left) ;
Brill dressed as Santa Claus at Peddlers Village (right)

Mike Brill

authorHOUSE®

AuthorHouse™
1663 Liberty Drive
Bloomington, IN 47403
www.authorhouse.com
Phone: 1 (800) 839-8640

Published by AuthorHouse 06/20/2019

ISBN: 978-1-7283-1649-9 (sc)
ISBN: 978-1-7283-1647-5 (hc)
ISBN: 978-1-7283-1648-2 (e)

Library of Congress Control Number: 2019908124

Print information available on the last page.

This book is printed on acid-free paper.

CONTENTS

For more pictures and information about the author
and the book please visit Facebook Page:
Hello My Name Is Santa@MikeVBrill

Email: **Hellomynameissanta603@gmail.com**

Names have been changed in this story

Energy

THE STRENGTH AND VITALITY REQUIRED FOR SUSTAINED PHYSICAL OR MENTAL ACTIVITY

CHAPTER 1

Everything Is Ok

As I strolled along the southeast coast of Bali, Indonesia, I was mutually nervous and wide eyed with excitement and wonderment. While my toes dragged the waters of the third ocean, I've seen in my world travels, the Indian Ocean, my life changed for the better. At that time, I just didn't honestly know how to embrace it fully. I couldn't.

Stepping on white pebbles in the wet sand and salty water didn't bother me today. Neither was I afraid of the ocean or its inhabitants. Lombok, one of the 922 inhabited islands in Indonesia's archipelago, was off to my left kissing the new day's sunrise on the horizon. My tears met the Indian Ocean. Salt kissed salt. The beaches were empty and quiet in the early morning. Soon, paradise beach travelers would emerge and congregate on their respective resort beach boundaries, soaking in a different kind of sun. I was practically on the equator and the sun burns differently and more dangerously, especially for this Irish pale-skinned American. At this early hour in the morning, I was brave and denied myself the protection of my SPF 15, 30 or 50. Today, for once in my life, I was a beach person.

A bit earlier that morning, upon waking up on my first day in Bali, to the tropical morning darkness, I quietly left my hotel room and descended to the beach to witness the sun rise. Jet lag, 2 days of travel or nothing else would inhibit me from witnessing my first day's sunrise over the Indian Ocean. I didn't pay a dime or an Indonesian Rupiah for this excursion. The white sands welcomed me.

I nestled down on the first lounge chair I could find. I sat and could only tear up. The tears fell and heightened my awareness. Different birds chirp in this country. The wind blows with mysterious temperatures. I heard a foreign language in my head, but not a person was present. Serenity and peace are delivered in one language. I sat wondering if this is the same sun that rises over Philadelphia and how that can be possible. I asked questions; while reveling in not needing to know the answers. I was high on life. In sobriety, I call them earned freebies.

I took myself 10,000 miles away from home for this moment. The sky began changing, inventing colors that are not found in a 64 pack of Crayola crayons. Bob Ross would have blushed. In chorus, the sun winked over the horizon and tears flowed down my cheeks. Hyperventilation began. I stopped trying to stop it. In coordination, the sun rose and tears cascaded in harmony with the beauty from which I was surrounded. I held onto the lounge chair, over the next 15 minutes, gripping it as if I was approaching the first downward fall of a roller coaster ride. It was a Balinese sunrise all for me.

Brill First Bali Sunrise

My hotel began serving breakfast shortly after the sun rose. The breakfast fruit fell off the tree, sliced in perfect shapes. Freshness at its finest. Hospitality workers appeared, dressed in kitchen attire that somehow maintained a consistency with the local clothing. I decided my day was just starting and opted to eat later, after the walk.

The ocean stroll was surreal. On this ceremonious walk, I had no schedule or destination and that was a good thing. Time didn't matter. A walking meditative greeting to the country I've come to love and respect was the only mission. It became my baptism.

After stopping and starting my walk a couple hundred times, attempting to look for a pause button on my life and views, I came across a group of Balinese teenagers sitting in a circle around a diminishing bonfire. I wasn't sure if they were there all night or just starting their day. They laughed and spoke Balinese and with my less than mediocre local language skills only catching a few stray words. *Selamat Pagi* came out of my mouth. And they returned with the same salutation; slipping in a few chuckles. They recognized my American accent in saying "Good Morning" to them in Balinese. They invited me over and welcomed me to their group.

As I walked over, one of the teenagers reached around a log and brought out a guitar. My eyes lit up. The guitar had cracks with other vivid deterioration. The strings were old. It didn't have a brand name announcing its creator. I ignored my status of being a Martin Guitar owner. I was staying in the moment, coming to the realization that this guitar was the most beautiful instrument I have ever seen in my life.

I listened to my new friend play a few songs with the others singing along in Balinese. Some got up and danced. Momentary glances and giggles erupted in my direction from my new posse. I tried to sing a few bars and lyrics. Determined for participation, I settled on clapping, while crying. The tear ducts were full, but emptying quickly. Can tears dry up?

My new friend then offered me the guitar. After a quick denial, shaking my head and waving my hands, the guitar was quickly on my thigh, under my shoulder, leaning against my stomach. I strummed my first chord in Bali, Indonesia. A chord to be determined later, as nervousness trumped my guitar skills. I couldn't think of a single song to play. The experience alone was endearing and winning. I simply embraced the moment and my new friendships.

After noodling on the guitar for a bit and feeling the pressure of my new friends' anticipation, I began to sing, Irish singer-songwriter Luka

Bloom's song: *Don't Be Afraid of the Light That Shines Within You.* The song's message is simply what is in the title. It says it all. It's my anthem to better myself and encourage other's the same. It became the most appropriate song, encapsulating my morning sunrise stroll and meeting with strangers, now friends, welcoming the light of another into their small group. Sources of humanistic kindness consumed me. I sang it loud and passionately. The light was shining. Though some of them may not have understood the words, it appeared the message of the song was fully embraced by each of them. Smiles and clapping don't evolve from any dictionary. At that moment, in my personal time and space, everything was O.K.

A long time ago, in the early fall of 2002, five years prior to my sober Balinese voyage, I staggered down the street after closing a neighborhood bar. At 2am, it was the fifth or sixth bar I was in that day, always searching for the next good time. Actually, I was constantly thinking I was missing something that might be going on somewhere else.

I was having difficulty staying on the pavement as I grabbed onto air to steady myself. I approached the street I use to live on for the past year and a half. Turning down that street and going to that house was no longer an option. I was no longer welcome. I passed by friends' houses and familiar backyards and decks. Many a night I would sneak, climb and invade various backyard locations for my shelter for the night. I often awoke in the morning to friends and/or family members wondering why Mike Brill was sleeping on their patio furniture on the deck. Sometimes I miscalculated and slept in a stranger's backyard. If they had patio furniture, I was content.

Tonight was different. My ego and escalating embarrassment of such occasions pulled me further away from people in my staggering search for a bed, shelter and survival. I approached the traffic light intersection and jaywalked across the street, towards the park. At this intersection, Pennypack Park, in Northeast Philadelphia, had an entrance to the bike trail that was buried in the trees and foliage. There was no entrance sign present. Only locals know of this entrance. In the thick darkness and remaining fall foliage of the end of summer caused this local drunk to almost give up his search. Finally, I found it and proceeded down the dirt and cobblestone hill towards the trail and creek. The alcohol, incline and gravity made this a perilous trek. Halfway down the hill an old stone wall on my left side became my crutch and salvation in staying vertical and physically unharmed.

After reaching the bottom safely I stared straight ahead towards the still creek. There were small waterfalls that I could vaguely hear trickling off in the distance. The creek was stocked with fish a few times a season. That ceremony brought local city folk out of their concrete jungle into a different ecological world, declaring themselves anglers for a few hours. Fathers and sons standing across from beer guzzling construction workers equally found solace in this urban forested creek. The waterfalls became a liquid playground for teenagers. Health conscious people ran, walked and biked along the path. There was no one there tonight at 2:45am. Tonight, it was my bedroom without a roof.

I was homeless.

At that moment, I did not dare call myself homeless. I was simply looking for sleep and survival, without judgement. After a few seconds, thanking God I made it down the hill safely and staring into the creek, I turned right towards the amphitheater. An open grass field with a slight incline, ran down towards a huge cement stage. I remember hearing about my older brother's band and other musical acts performing there in the 1970's and 80's. It had been barren and useless for many years. Although, tonight I would be performing. If only for me.

Walking along the trail, off to my left, was a bridge to other trails and a series of parking lots. Back in the day, it was called "Little City." Its where young people parked their cars after dark to conclude their date, say long goodnights, break up or lose their virginity. I sat down by the edge of the creek and stared across at the parking lot. I thought about the hearts I had broken and the beautiful intimate relationships I had destroyed in my addictions. I unavoidably reminisced about my present loneliness and the time I lost my virginity, which was not in that parking lot. My eyes became very heavy and filled with tears. To avoid my sad memories, I laid back in the dewy grass and passed out.

I awoke freezing cold, as the alcohol numbness was extinguished and the early fall elements became piercing. I got up staggering looking for the larger leaves that populated that area of the park to cover me like a blanket and keep me warm. Each leaf I picked up was more wet than the other.

It then dawned on me, that maybe I should continue my trek to the Ed Kelly Amphitheater Stage. After walking another 500 yards, I stood on the cement dance floor in front of the stage. It was brighter in this area of the park as the moon and stars could penetrate through the treeless, open aired space. I took a running start at the stage and hoped up on one try. It was actually not as smooth as it sounded. I ran chest first into the cement stage and lifted my right leg up on the stage, like I was hoping a fence. I scraped my chin and cold knee, while proceeding to slowly pull the rest of my soaked body up onto the stage. As I lay on my back on the stage, I was thankful no one saw me. Blood trickled from my new wounds.

I decided not to sleep right there on the front part of the stage, as I didn't want to scare the morning park attendees. It wouldn't be the first time concerned citizens called 911 in light of finding me passed out in public on their property. I stood up on the stage and looked out on the open moonlit field and imagined hundreds of people cheering. There was only one thing left to do: AIR GUITAR. I began strumming an air guitar, swinging my arm around windmill style, just like Pete Townshend of The Who. I even started singing Baba O'Reilly at the top of my lungs. "Teenage wasteland…..we're ALL WASTED" I sang. I was exhausted in less than a minute, running from one end of the stage to the other, being sure I was entertaining everyone in the crowd that didn't exist that night.

That was my only performance on that stage and I still dream of performing there someday, in front of real people. It's one of my musical goals. The stage has been resurrected by local community leaders and hosts concerts every Wednesday night during the summer months.

That night, after walking by the steps leading up to the stage that I wished I knew existed five minutes ago, I went back stage. In the rear of the stage stood cement walls that back up to the creek. Tonight, with some semi dry ultra big leaves I crawled up in the fetal position and fell off to sleep.

I awoke relieved no one saw me. There were bikers flying by on the trail, frisbee throwers in the field and fishing lines in the creek. All of them hanging on to what was left of the summer of 2002. I had no plan and finally admitted to myself, I was homeless. The firm and harsh reality pierced me like the elements throughout the night.

I wandered back down the trail towards the undeclared exit, that was my entrance last night. I slowly walked up the stony incline, again thankful I didn't fall in my staggering arrival. I walked through a tree archway towards the world I didn't want to face. I thought about getting help, but soon reached into my pocket preferring and hoping I had a few dollars for a pint of beer to start my day. At 10:15am, I had $12 left and found great joy in that unconscious money management decision of the previous night.

As I approached the intersection, a jogger, an old neighborhood friend, startled me, asking: "Yo Mikey Brill, what's up, how you doing buddy?" Hoping no one saw me that morning, riddled with the truthful reality of homelessness, my safe response stammered: "I'm O.K.!"

I was always O.K., no matter what. Nothing more, nothing less and onto the next binge I rambled.

At the equator of human emotional existence lies O.K. My life in addictions and early sobriety existed at the equator. It was my safest response to life inquiries. Everything, all the time, was O.K., in avoidance of revealing my reality, possibly creating vulnerability or further responsibility of explanation.

To exhibit the contrast to my truthful realties, I was also O.K. being homeless. While, my first morning experiences on the beaches of Bali I considered O.K. It was not O.K, it was fucking awesome. At 4 years sober, I still couldn't let myself properly measure the truest value of my personal emotional and physical experiences. I often wondered, that day in Bali, whether I was worthy of such blessings, even as they were occurring.

Over time, especially in Bali, I learned to truthfully measure internal and external realities. I commenced to feel worthy of physical and emotional exploration in order to warrant its truest effect on my life. Providing myself permission to feel those moments in Bali, the trip becomes more majestic and one of the most amazing experiences in my life. Equally, the extent of the insanity and danger in being homeless should also be assessed in order to become a lesson towards where I don't want my life to end up.

Measurement is responsibility. Now, I measure frequently and honestly.

CHAPTER 2

Big League Victim

As a child growing up, I was very active in sports. Baseball, basketball, football, soccer and golf were my major sports. I would play every variation of these type sports in my alley, schoolyard or playground. Every season of the year was consumed with formal team games and practices. Having three older brothers with the same active sporting agendas kept my mom and dad on their toes, to the point I often wondered if they had clones. They attended almost every game. Sometimes, Mom and Dad had to split forces with one parent attending my game; while, one of my brothers was blessed to have the other parent in the stands rooting them onto victory. If my parents couldn't make a game, I remember an ongoing heartfelt apology, coupled with a detailed explanation of the reasons why they would not be in attendance. They were rarely guilty of omission. This explanation and apology were appreciated but not necessary. As a child, the fruits of their parenting skills fell to the wayside. It was only appreciated fully, later in my life.

Brill with Mom and Dad - 6 months old (1970)

Mom became the greatest short order cook, serving meals on the fly, as if the bottoms of her feet had roller blades. Mom had a turnaround in meals that would make George Jetson blush as he pressed a button for his next meal to appear fully prepared. Mom even had a short order menu ranging from breakfast for dinner with my favorite being poached eggs over white toast, pork roll and cheese, to a spaghetti feast. Whether it was leftovers reheated or a freshly made sandwich, mom's lasting ingredient was her altruistic pinches of love and care for her sons. It was compounded by her mutual ongoing enthusiasm for our diet and sporting activities.

Additionally, mom had a full dinner menu and some of my fondest memories were all six of us sitting at a small kitchen table eating dinner together - A rare blessing seldom experienced or found in today's family and work structure. The demands of vital double income households have robbed our world of this lasting tradition.

Neighbors considered the Brill brothers to be the most obedient boys. As Mom yelled "dinner time" we immediately came running, dropping bats in mid swing or forgetting there was even a game being played. What the neighbors didn't know was that mom cooked enough for everyone. No one was lacking their nutrients or fill for the night. However, when at the dinner table, it became a riot fest of who could eat the most and the fastest. We often spoke about renting our brother out to a freak show or carnival to have people simply watch him eat. We often merely asked him to breathe, while dad just shook his head in disbelief. My parents knew what to say and do in almost every situation. Oftentimes, their greatest strategy of conquest was sitting back and choosing their battles wisely, often succeeding while doing or saying nothing.

My mother had an intuition and art of questioning skills that could out match any FBI agent. My father didn't beat around the bush and gave it to me straight. Mom and Dad's opposing parenting strategies were often the spark of a tiff between the two of them. As the youngest child, I realized being the baby had its privileges. Of course, I took full advantage of those benefits as frequently as possible. I remember ignoring my parent's intuitiveness. After all, I was about 12 years old and was close to knowing everything. Plus, I had Philadelphia Phillies legend Mike Schmitt as one of my role models and there was nothing that was going to stop me from playing on the Phillies.

Baseball was quickly becoming my number one sport in achievement and enjoyment. I performed well in the others sports; but there was something about America's pastime, the smell of the leather, crack of the bats and perfect weather that lured me into focusing on baseball. Ironically, I began my passion with golf a few years earlier, age 9, with my dad teaching me the basics in a concrete back yard in Northeast Philadelphia.

Kind of a funny place to golf. It certainly wasn't a country club. I call it the Concrete Country Club (CCC), a place where a father, against all odds, created a bonding and teaching environment of the sport he loved and adored his entire life. Only a father could create such a time and place. My father would place a square carpet remnant on the cement ground and place plastic golf balls down, teaching me the basics of swinging a golf club. Hitting the plastic balls straight into the face of the back of our house. Frequently, a stray ball landed in the neighbor's yard. Those shanks created opportunity for more teaching. Dad never hesitated to seize the moment. Each time I golf today, I reflect on those lessons from Dad. I tell the story every chance I get. Later in life, during high school, due to baseball and golf taking place in the same season, I had to choose to play one or the other. I chose golf. Maybe, this is why?

I always found my way on the baseball diamo
third basemen, second basemen, short-stop, pitcher (
baseman, after I threw my elbow out throwing curve
developmental years on the mound. I began every sᴇᴀ
championship trophy. I also became fixated on walking of the stage a
annual Moss sports banquet, at Four Chefs Catering Hall, with the smaller
trophy, declaring me the MVP – Most Valuable Player. Moss Athletic
Association, where I played my sports, was a reputable organization with
some of the most amazing athletic talent I've ever witnessed in my life.
Coaches and players had high expectations at the start of every sporting
season.

During a few of my baseball games in early season, I noticed an older
man in the stands enthusiastically cheering home teams on and giving
individual compliments acknowledging achievement. His compliments
reflected knowledge of the sport and made me feel like I was playing on a
different level. At age 6, I dreamed of the Big Leagues, now after doubling
my age, at age 12, I was receiving the compliments and acknowledgment,
from my coaches, teammates, parents and a new friend that revealed my
personal assumption that he could help that dream come true. Well, that
is what this 12-year-old heard.

After baseball practices or games, I would stay at the field and practice
with him and some other kids from the neighborhood. He knew the
history and stats of baseball like the back of his hand. The motivation,
compliments and encouragement kept coming. I felt like I was obtaining
that extra ingredient of skill and esteem to make my dream come true.

One day, in a side conversation, this new older friend asked me if I
knew what it would take to get into the big leagues. My response alluded to
hard work, practice, commitment, and sacrifice. Ignoring my responses, he
said two simple words reflecting a new skill: Switch Hitter. He stated that
being a switch hitter would increase my substance and chance to make it
to the big leagues. He alleged teams are always looking for talented switch
hitters because they are a vital pawn in the strategy of winning baseball
games, especially in the later innings. Baseball teams strategized with left
and right handed relief pitchers. A common response to this baseball tactic
was to use a switch hitter for the offensive. It made sense to me.

That day started my training. I began taking a swing from the right side of the plate and the next pitch from the other side of the plate, left-handed. As awkward and foreign as it felt, my new baseball coach and friend told me that memory of swinging right handed and going through that same motion, immediately afterwards, would improve my left-hand swing. Both swings work together and feed off of one another. It was true. I began cracking the baseball left-handed. Not ever as good as right handed; but I was improving. He reminded me I have plenty of years to work on this new skill and make it to the big leagues.

Along with some other kids in the neighborhood, our friendship grew as we surrounded ourselves and followed this man, yearning to learn and grow in the sport of baseball. This was my ticket to the big leagues. Only one thing hindered my pathway and lessons towards a tryout for the Phillies. My mother's intuition and my father's downright concern grew and soon became verbalized pleas for me to stop hanging out with my new friend. "I just don't like him and there's something about him" they would say. I would respond with "oh mom/dad this is my chance for the big leagues….he's a great person and my new friend…..don't worry about it."

Our sad days were when it rained and the baseball diamond at Moss A.A. became a swamp. The solitary dirt infield of the diamond at Moss A.A. had no drainage and became victim of flooding during a sun shower. Luckily, our new friend had a ping pong table in his garage, at his home, just a few short blocks from our field of dreams. I was also learning this activity or sport of ping-pong and became very good. Later in college, I become the dorm champion in ping pong. This being one of my only achievements in early attempts at higher education.

All of us young kids would take turns trying to beat him. We seldom found victory. On occasion, when you thought he was letting you win, he turned the tables quickly, slamming one shot after another to come back and be victorious after he was losing for most of the game. It was rare that anyone beat him. We only found victory in table tennis when the kids played against each other. After all, one of us had to win.

The day came when he offered to take a car load of us kids down to the beach for the day. Swim in the ocean, walk along the boardwalk and take in the Wildwood, New Jersey sunshine. He told me: while working hard and focusing on the Big Leagues, it was also important to have some fun.

As the wildwood summer hazy moon arose over the boardwalk, this man had a couple of tired kids on his hands. The ocean frolicking, beach games and walking miles on the boardwalk would do anyone in, especially pre-teens and teenagers. On our last trek down the boardwalk and back to the car, one of the older kids was more than tired. He became recluse or maybe even angry, not saying a word all the way home. Something was concerning him and weighed heavy on his mind. It was more than being denied ice cream. It was a silent ride home. I assumed the silence was from the long Wildwood day. At times, it appeared awkward. In my 12 year old prized opinion, the day was a success.

I slept sound that night and dreamed of my first at bats at Veterans Stadium, in the Big Leagues, wearing a #20 Philadelphia Phillies jersey. That is, if they didn't retire Schmidty's #20 before my big-league debut.

Later that week, after our Wildwood excursion, I rode my bike past the playground, dodging my age appropriate friends, who were playing basketball, football or hide-the-belt, straight to my new "friend's" house. I parked my bike in the yard, went in the back door and he was practicing ping pong, by himself. He had a make shift practice board set up that would return the ball back to him. He welcomed me with a smile and immediately challenged me to a game. I assume his solitude and boredom of hitting the ping pong ball to himself got old a few hours ago.

As I embarked on this challenge, I focused on his one golden rule of ping-pong. He always fervently instructed that when I get into trouble, during a volley, always return the ball to the opponent's center line. Never go on the offensive or attempt to win a point when your back is up against the wall. I felt fully prepared and ready for the challenge.

It was a different kind of game where I was beating him most of the game. At moments during the game, it felt like a battle. Other times it felt like a joke to him. He would loft his shots up in the air; to the point where a monkey could have returned the shot and won the point. He was the person who taught me the game and he knew my skills were better than his ridiculous efforts against me. I won 2 of 3 games. I did not feel victorious. I was actually pissed off in winning that way. It was a teasing, pity win. Not earned.

He was acting differently, as we were alone in his basement reflecting on his defeat and my cheesy victory. We aimlessly talked about sports and sometimes went back to specific shots and tactics of our ping pong match. It was unorganized conversation. It appeared he was verbally admitting, in a roundabout way, his flagrant, strategic skills in letting me win. Out of nowhere, he broke the awkward reflection by asking me if I wanted to see a magic trick. Now, I have gotten plenty of magic hats, cards and kits as a child, but never became very good and usually lost interest in the art of this skill and entertainment by Christmas night. His magic changed my life forever.

He used the same magic trick on me twice; both times in order to have me do something. He asked me how much I wanted to bet, that the next card he flipped over would be my card. As I saw my card on the table already discarded, my response was I will bet you a million dollars. As the deck of cards sat in his left hand palm, his right hand went over to the top of the deck to signify he was going to turn over the top card. I felt assured that the top card was not mine because my card had already been discarded and "knew" I would win the bet. After reducing the wager to 50 cents, he pulled his hand away from the deck of cards, reached into the discard pile and flipped over my card. I was blown away and baffled. I immediately wanted to know how he did the trick. He stated that magicians do not reveal their secrets or do a trick twice in order to leave the audience hanging in bewilderment and thoroughly entertained. After my begging and pleading to learn the trick, he agreed to do the trick again. I thought there was no way he could possibly achieve this trick again. While going for double or nothing, I was ignoring the basic fundamentals of magic; that the truth and answer lie in the magician, even before the trick begins. The magician is always in control.

That man, my "friend", who taught me ping pong, sports trivia, riding waves in the ocean and most of all, wanted me to make it to the big leagues. My "friend" who was doing everything in his power to teach and motivate me to become a star switch hitter. He said I could someday play for the Phillies. On that day, instead of paying the double or nothing wager on the second attempt of the magic trick, that animal began teaching me about the male anatomy, tricking me through magic, into having me touch him.

Groomed and manipulated, I froze and did as I was told. On that day, I became a Big-League Victim and into my box of trauma I went.

I now knew what happened to my friend that day in Wildwood. It's the only explanation. I became a shadow of a hole, just like my friend in Wildwood. Robbed of my innocence, my life would never be the same. Trauma often has a way of dealing a new deck of cards to the individual victimized. At that moment, I went into a tunnel with my new, traumatic set of 52 cards. It completely changed my view of self and the world. I doubted my own identity and became mad at the world. I didn't run. I couldn't. I couldn't cry. I wouldn't. I could do nothing but the thing that this sick animal tricked me into doing to him. I was so scared, while wishing I listened to Mom and Dad. They were right all along.

On that bike ride home, I prayed no one would see me. I rode my bike to Moss playground and St. Bartholomew's School, familiar sanctuaries of safe space, but strategized through terror to avoid any familiar faces. I cried the entire time, as I circled blocks trying to figure out what just happened. I purposely got lost in my own neighborhood, on the streets I knew my entire life. I rode my bike for hours that afternoon. I didn't go home and avoided the entire world. I just kept peddling and sinking into the abyss of sexual abuse trauma.

This spiral, on the way home, immediately became filled with lies, justification, blame and sheer terror. Would my friends find out? Would my coaches cut me from future teams? Would I be permitted back into my Catholic grade school, St Bartholomew's? Is this front-page news material? Will the cops be involved? Am I gay now? I shouldn't have been there alone! It's my fault! The nuns and priests would definitely know. It than hit me. Oh my God, how could I ever go home? I didn't know how I would hide this Scarlet Letter when I walk into my home and face my parents. Did I look different? Would my mother's intuition figure this out? My father? How could I even look him in the eye ever again?

When I made it home, successfully avoiding everyone and everything, I did what any trauma victim does and suppressed it, boxing it up in the vault with only one lock. I had the key. To persuade my parents, I ignored the most horrible thing that ever happened in my short life. I hoped my Academy Award worthy role, acting like nothing just happened to me, would surpass and triumph over my mom and dad's intuitive parental skills. I lost so much that day, but succeeded in sealing my vault. No winners in this game.

Time is a distraction and does not heal all. Humans heal. Or at least I hoped.

Over the days, weeks and months after being molested, I made the dark decision to not tell my parents. I was completely embarrassed of what happened. Not to mention, I did not heed their countless warnings of this man I called a "friend" who was my ticket to the big leagues. To not draw attention to this situation, my logical plan had me returning to that house of trauma.

In my mind, I couldn't just pull away from this man. I kept the façade of "friendship" going. If I stopped, changed or ceased the friendship in any way, my parents would know something is wrong. They would ask me questions and eventually see remnants of my Scarlet Letter that I attempted to wash off a thousand times in the shower. The cost of this decision was to be molested again and again. Each step back into that house, slipped me deeper into my trauma. Quantity does not necessarily determine severity in trauma. It only had to happen once. Mine continued. Everything I did was to keep this a secret. My parents went to their graves not knowing this happened to me. I figure and hope now they know. Although, I am not sure what that would do for me.

Bringing the darkness into light just makes more sense when trying to improve your personal view of self and the world. In darkness trauma festers. The light, through a constructive narrative, brings healing. I look at this trauma today with identity, as a counselor, person in long term recovery and most of all as an adult, who is still the son of Dot and Joe.

On certain days, I still take blame and embarrassing fault for this horror. Those are the days I remember I am thinking like a sexually abused 12-year-old, not a 49-year-old professional counselor and a good person who has searched and found instruments of healing. Nonetheless, I am and will always be a victim. Through sobriety, family, friends and self-care, I am a survivor. Healing never ends, because trauma does not disappear.

The greatest introduction to self is through adversity.

Does trauma cause substance use disorders? About 50 to 66% who suffer from PTSD, also are treated for Substance Use Disorders. My professional experience has revealed a much higher rate of 80 to 90% substance use disorder client's experienced severe and multiple episodes of trauma. I am careful when considering this causality as my addictions' explanation. I am on an eternal pursuit for explanations, as they bring forth peace, serenity and understanding. I've created excuses most of my life. Excuses are unproductive, selfish constructs that leave a person in their own war of internal and external deliberations and confusion.

Here is my addiction story.

CHAPTER 3

The Perfect Storm

I grew up turning double plays on Moss Athletic Association's baseball diamond and turning around to look at the "old heads" playing basketball, drinking quarts of beer from a brown paper bag. They were having fun. I just assumed that was my next stage.

I grew up in an Irish Catholic family, with drinking and parties frequently on the agenda. I naturally assumed controlled drinking was my future. I grew up with friends that also had older brothers and we just followed in their footsteps. Social normalization can be deceiving, especially in an era of little education or awareness of alcoholism and addiction. Drinking alcohol and the decision itself are natural ingredients to human development. The choice of partaking in alcohol and drug is its own stage of decision-making models for most everyone. I didn't plan on being alcoholic, addicted or homeless. I didn't realize the responsibility that came with drinking and I certainly didn't know about alcoholism. To me, alcoholics were long-haired, un-showered, bearded men, wearing three trench coats, grasping at a paper bag, living under the I-95 bridge in Center City Philadelphia. Stereotypes and stigmas discriminate the truth.

On the night of my high school graduation party, at my house, I opened up a door that I could not close for 15 years. My drinking was escalating and progressing during high school. I thought: Doesn't everyone do it? It was just what I was supposed to be doing, as a teenager.

That night, as my party proceeded joyously, commemorating my scholastic accomplishment, I remembered there was another graduation party close by in my neighborhood. Another graduate was also celebrating his achievement with family and friends. I decided to leave the luxury and blessing of my own family and friends to stroll over to the party and see how the festivities were going and to share my accomplishment with other graduates. I walked in the back door and the small gathering of people told me that most people were in the garage. I backtracked, lifted the garage door and was welcomed by other celebrating graduates. Still to this day, I don't remember who was there.

I was quickly distracted with a first ever invite. Lying on the table among dips, drinks and chips were lines of cocaine – the door I opened that night. Quickly without hesitation I was offered to partake. I went cold and numb. I was scared. I was confused. I pondered, was this next on the developmental normalization scale of what I am supposed to do? I refused immediately, content in having my very own red Silo cup filled with beer. I was a big beer drinker in high school. During my business class my Senior Year we were assigned a stock market project where each student chose a business to track on the stock market to learn it firsthand. I chose Anheuser Busch as my company. My ongoing joke was that my drinking would help influence this stock in positive ways. I think back and wonder if I was half kidding.

Looking back, as a sober person thirsting for explanations, I truly believe my mind was an alcoholic first. I sat in academic classes, succeeding with very little effort. I was an academic natural, graduating in the top 10% of my graduating class. During daily classes, my thoughts raced as to whose parents were going away on vacation, how we were getting beer or what playground was holding the keg party. I was consumed with weekend partying. Friends, golf and good grades couldn't stop this cognitive runaway freight train. I drank heavily and differently than others. By the end of the night, I would be only wearing a red Silo cup in my hand, with maybe sneakers, so I could run when the cops came to break up the party. Drunk and naked was the story and tradition of my weekends in high school. I left nothing to the imagination.

In that garage, on graduation party night, I was not subjected to peer pressure, nor was I made to feel less than anyone, by anyone from my decision to refuse cocaine. I made my decision in an instant. "No, I'm good." My decision was welcomed and accepted by everyone.

A personally constructed wave of justification and rationalization came over me in an instant. It was consumed with the idea that I earned the right to experience something new in my life. I'm a graduate. I'm 18. What would one little line do to me? In a flash it became my "next." A rolled-up dollar bill was quickly affixed to my nose. I leaned over at a 90-degree angle, pushed closed my left nostril, opened up the entrance vacuum of the other nostril and instantly, this white powdery substance became a necessary instrument of my life over the next 15 years. It progressed in lies, deceit and despair. Like a dictator, the cocaine became my own personal governing body; declaring what I would do, where I would go and who with.

Brill with Mom and Dad 1988 North Catholic High School Graduation

After all of the numerous graduation festivities, among fellow graduates, my closest high school friends, the people I could not have made it through high school without, departed on a Floridian Senior Week. As the majority of Philadelphia graduating seniors, including my girlfriend at the time, departed for Wildwood N.J., we decided to do something different and a little more special. We embarked for a special engagement with Mickey Mouse and his friends at Disney World.

Kissimmee, Florida was invaded by 16 Falcons of the North Catholic's graduating class of 1988. One of the bathroom tubs was designated as the cooler. It was stocked for 7 days straight with assortments of beer. Fake ID's and an alcohol selling deli within walking distance of the hotel, supplied our demand for the week.

We partook in everything Florida, the hotel and Disney World had to offer. Prioritizing scheduled beer runs to the deli. Mornings and afternoons by the pool and day long excursions to the parks: Disney World and newly constructed EPCOT – Experimental Prototype Community of Tomorrow. In 7th grade, my family made the Disney trip and EPCOT was just being built. It was all the rage during our trip. Me and my brother would continually quiz my father on what EPCOT stood for. I'm not sure he ever got it right in his lifetime. However, my brother and I cracked up every time he struggled trying to solve the age-old riddle, inventing a new word for each letter. I liked Dad's defined acronyms better.

In EPCOT, all of the major countries of the world were represented and this gave us a feeling of a global trek, all while roaming in a single zip code. We adapted to each culture, enriching our lives and entertaining others'. One of our friends played the guitar. While in Sweden, the typical blond, beautiful Swedish female playing the guitar at the entrance was enveloped by a gaggle of hungover high school graduates. Within a blink of an eye, the guitar was around our friend's neck with our whole crowd singing "shake it up baby, shake it up baby, twist and shout, twist and shout." Sweden was now our dominion and we ruled it with song, dance and laughter. I often wonder how we didn't meet more representatives of the local legal authorities. It truly was a drink fest and for me it ended wrong.

I look back on the end of that week and I shudder to think how stupidly I reacted to my friends' drunken and harmless prank they played on me. I wish I could go back and speak to myself, that stupid over-reacting, drunk and immature 18-year-old kid. The details of the prank are not important but what was prioritized, for me, was my validation to walk away from the greatest friends, that I called brothers, for the past 4 years of my life. I could never imagine my high school years or present days without these friends. Time, space and new families could never break our bond. But I let it for a while. On that trip, I personalized something that was strictly born out of pure drinking fun. Everyone in high school had their turn and on that Senior Week my ticket was pulled. The joke was on me. I became bitter and isolated.

The last two days were lonely for me. I drank, stayed drunk and kept quiet, after pillaging and wrecking a hotel room in reaction to the prank. I went on a lone excursion to Sea World, finding myself penniless upon exiting the park. I called home for sympathy, but to no avail. It just rang. I hitched hiked back to the hotel room and thankfully a sane human being, concerned for a teenage kid walking along the interstate, picked me up. My first and only experience of hitchhiking was a success. Like an immature person, I did not speak to those friends for many years. I used them to open up more doors that I could not close. Poor me, poor me, POUR ME ANOTHER!

Upon departing from the quiet plane ride home to Philadelphia, I was greeted by my parents and girlfriend at the airport. I walked by them and said "C'mon let's go home." They were baffled, as I pulled them away from my friends' parents who became my parent's friends over the years of friendships established during high school. I pleaded my case on the ride home. For the next several months, in order to cement my rationalization in my favor and decrement of a true justification, I created more ingredients manipulating my story. It kept me sick, stagnated in my own pity and misery.

Back at my house, I went through the story again, with my girlfriend, continually looking for pity, in the hopes of building my "Mike Brill Brigade" against those so-called friends of mine. The perfect storm raged on when instead of pity, I got the Dear John Monologue from my girlfriend breaking up with me. Senior weeks had a way of erasing many realities in our young lives, forcing us to grow up sooner rather than later. I did not grow up. One does not mature when consumed with concern of accumulating others' pity. My solution became substances and plenty of them.

The summer of 1988, at 18 years of age, became the rationalized decision and pursuit into the abyss of addictions. I made the decision to drink alcohol every day. Poor me wanted to "show" everyone. It didn't matter if I had plans. Somehow and some way, I would obtain at least a 6 pack of beer each night for consumption. It was a consciously constructed layout and plan with blueprints. I put the plan into daily motion fervently and consistently. I found more beer on most nights and soon found that substance that I was looking for the most.

I found people that were partaking and had easy access to garage table party favors. Alcohol and cocaine fed off each other. It helped me drink more. It made me socialize more. Nothing else mattered for a very long time.

My partial scholarships for NCAA golf went to seed. I dropped the ball on every opportunity of Higher Education that my four years of scholastic and athletic efforts once provided. I was going somewhere during high school. But the only place I found myself that summer was "down the way" obtaining more cocaine. I was missing and partying for days at a time. I have been robbed, beaten physically and financially by dealers, and had guns pointed at my head. Once, I heard the click of the trigger, followed by the gunman stating: "stupid, white boy." My head stayed collapsed between my legs for an hour, while shaking uncontrollably. After an hour of trauma, the party was back on. I returned repeatedly "down the way" each time I wanted and needed more; no matter what the possible outcomes could reveal.

After that summer of '88, I settled for a year in community college. I would save money, obtain my general education courses and then go away to college; pursuing golf and a major in Business Management. My goal of being a golf professional slowly became a figment of my imagination, throughout my first year of college. My rounds of golf that year calculated to zero, as my greens fee funds became an investment in white powdery purchases. Those drug purchases robbed me of my development in the game of golf and so much more. I was pissing on the carpet remnants that my dad laid out to teach me the game of the golf. My aspirations to become something or anything dwindled. I went on till there was nothing left of me. I was broke and broken in one short year. My parents knew something was going on.

Despite my realities and progression of addictions, with the assistance of my parents, as they often did, I transferred up to a state school in the Pennsylvania Poconos. The golf coach strongly encouraged me to attend and I received some financial assistance to transfer and play golf, starting in my sophomore year. In the fall of 1989, I got my wish to transfer away from home and truly begin my life in pursuit all of my goals. The only problem that existed was that I needed to take myself with me. The doors were ajar and they were doors that I could not close for 15 years. College promoted and reinforced this reality.

CHAPTER 4

Higher Education - W.A.L.S.T.I.B.

I was a member of an NCAA sports team playing golf and was invited to pledge a fraternity, during my first semester at college. A transfer student is considered eligible for pledging during their first semester of Sophomore year. The two realities of sports and social fraternity were the perfect prescription to continue my diabolical patterns of feeding my addiction. I thought, wasn't this next and what every college student does? My normalization continued.

School quickly became a façade to only help procure my bodily existence on campus. My dorm roommate was a junior and already a member of the fraternity. He became my Big Brother. Our passion for the same music and social constructs ignited a friendship that still exists today. Eventually, even his concern for my drinking surfaced.

Pledging was one of the greatest things I ever did in life, but I would never do again. Thankfully, I do not have to. Once a brother always a brother. I found a unique and everlasting association in brothers and other members of social organizations that still exists. When I told people that I was pledging this particular fraternity, their responses ranged from complete silence to a shiver of fear and concern. Many, just shook their heads. It was a grueling physical and mental pathway to brotherhood.

Pledging ignited a new reality and philosophy of life that I sustain even today. It's an ingredient of my spirituality and work ethic. There truly is a bond that can occur with people that I did not know for 19 years of my life. Dedication and achievement occurred on that morning after a 15-hour Hell Night, the last night of pledging.

Hell Week is just that: HELL. It's amazing to partake in realizing the parameters of stretched boundaries of individual potential that occurs in a pledge becoming a brother. As I survived each daunting task, getting through one more day of that relentless week, a fire ignited in me through the aspiration to achieve something individually and collectively, with my fellow pledge brothers. For six weeks, in my first semester away at college, I found something I was missing since I walked away from my high school friends in Florida. As the sun was coming up over a portion of the Appalachian Trail, it was over. I achieved something qualitative. Furthermore, on that exhausting morning, I hugged men that just became my new brothers for a lifetime.

At the end of the semester, with golf and pledging demands overtaking my academia, I was happy to have a number to the left of the decimal point in my GPA. A whopping 1.25 GPA appeared on my transcript. Academic probation for my second semester away at college.

My fraternity brotherhood contained every type of person. From muscle heads to Dead Heads, we created and maintained a unique and culturally diverse social population on campus. Our Greek letters bonded us all as we each went through the same pledging struggles, while ultimately sharing in the conquest of brotherhood. I gravitated toward the later population and soon found myself on tour, as frequently as possible, with the Grateful Dead. My work, school demands, and responsibilities went further down the scale of my prioritizations.

Cocaine became too rich but when it was around in college, I never refused an invite to partake. I soon replaced cocaine with hallucinogens, while my drinking escalated. These elements, LSD and Mushrooms, are the most powerful mind-altering substances on earth. I grew to love them and the alternative mind-expanding reality they provided; even despite my first *trip* experience.

Three of us had plans on going out to the see the local Grateful Dead cover band, *Willie and the Poor Boys*. They were performing at a local club, further up in the Poconos, *The El Coyote*. The pregame drinking expedition led to a short debate on whether or not to purchase and do mushrooms. Psilocybe cubensis was in town and my friends knew where to get them. Washing the magic mushrooms down with beer and bananas, gave way to the most amazing visuals that were bright and lasting. At the time, I had no idea of the power of these mushrooms.

I entered college as a connoisseur and passionate for 80's New Wave Music: The Smiths, The Cure, Echo and the Bunnymen, Red Hot Chili Peppers, Psychedelic Furs, Violent Femmes, and others filled 4 containers, each holding 100 cassettes. It was on dorm moving day, when my new roommate saw my cassettes come into the room. Immediately, he knew we would get along just fine. However, on this fall night, in the Poconos, I was initiated with melodies, rhythms and sounds that I never heard before from music.

After gagging and throwing up from my maiden fungus consumption, I uncontrollably laughed for what seemed hours. On the way to the show, the lights of the Pocono roads became ray beams and every hair on my body lifted with euphoria. Time stood still; while, simultaneously feeling like days passed. I assumed this is where the term tripping originated. I was getting "it."

We contained our laughter and strolled into the El Coyote, pupils fully dilated. The guitar's wa-wa pedal hurled trickling vibrations over the warm mushrooms running through my system. The music threw me into another dimension. The music wasn't loud. It was perfect. I heard every conversation over the music. Conversation complimented the music. For the first time, music became more than just sound. It declared space and time in harmony. Colorful tie-dyed shirts and hippie skirts twirled and grooved on the dance floor. Smiles, laughter and songs filled the air. We all permitted the music to fill the air. I had no choice. It was happening. Each person was dancing on their own, achieving their individual peace and groove, with a collective appreciation for the here and now. Every one of my senses were enlightened threefold. I immediately felt out of place, as I was dressed like Robert Smith of The Cure. A solitary color of black draped me in my night's clothing choice. What was I thinking?

After settling in with some alcohol, beer was my go-to relaxer, I sat back and took in the bar and vibe of the El Coyote. There were couches strewn perfectly over the country wooden floors. Curtains hung on the windows presenting me with a home-feel of a living room space. Between some of the couches stood fully set up chess boards. Some people were even engaged in a match. Not sure I could even pick up a pawn at that point of the night. The band performed in front of tied dye tapestries, as colorful as a rainbow. This rainbow moved with the music. Tonight, those colors became as mobile as a painter's brush. I yearned for one of those colors on my body. The visuals and trails of light, color and sound became concrete and quite overwhelming to this Grateful Dead and hallucinogen rookie.

As I took in the whole scene, I felt like the whole night was scripted and we were the players in this night's theatrical production. I knew only a few people and shortly followed, what I thought, was their lead to something grandeur. I guess I've always been a follower, rather than a leader. I feel I'm a perfectionist. A perfectionist should not bring their lofty goal of perfectionism onto a hallucinogen trip. Rather, they should accept themselves, and accept the perfection of the developing moments. This night, I didn't know any role in the production and shortly couldn't comprehend whether I was coming or going.

I didn't know how to dance by myself. At the time, that was simply a Billy Idol pop song, played too many times on MTV and the radio. Billy Idol wrote that song about a late night, on tour in Japan, as he cruised the night club scene. Around 4am, he went into a club and found single males literally dancing with themselves. Their reflection, in the mirrors on the wall, was there solitary dance partner.

I couldn't find my groove to the music, but something created a cosmic connection in my soul and with the communal of people sharing that night. I felt a freedom and solidarity. Although, it quickly became concerning, as my decisions weren't a part of the whole production. Or, so I thought.

The kitchen was surrounded by the U-shaped bar and I found myself, through my new-found freedom, wandering back behind the bar and into the kitchen for no apparent reason. I became a bit mute and my muffled conversation was not making any sense to myself or anyone. I simply created a new language, rooted in mumble. I can only imagine what the listeners and participants of my trip were thinking. I assumed that a track became attached under my feet, like the race car attached to the hand-controlled racing track of my childhood car game TCR (Total Control Racing). I simply let it take me anywhere, without any thoughts of consequences. I presumed there were no boundaries or limitations on mushrooms. The music provided a soundtrack to my personal decisions and actions. I simply let the music be my remote control, steering me aimlessly, however I lost the control and responsibility of this new freedom.

My friends shortly saw that this black sheep of his new hippie family, in his Robert Smith outfit, looked like he was having a bad trip. I turned to my friend, looked up at his 6' 6" head and said: "explain myself to me." That immediately became the mantra of Mike Brill's long trippy college career. W.A.L.S.T.I.B. - What a Long Strange Trip Its Been.

CHAPTER 5

The Bus Come By

On September 10, 1990, shortly after my second year away at college began and surviving academic probation, my hippie friends and I skipped out of school early and departed for Philadelphia. PA. At the legendary Spectrum, tonight would be my first time getting on the official bus of the Grateful Dead. "Getting on the bus" is a reference to being baptized in the vibration, music and family of the Grateful Dead. There is no formal ceremony. It's just an individual choice. Getting on the bus is simply the moment you fell in love with the Grateful Dead and all it creates and inspires. The phrase "getting on the bus" comes from band member, Grateful Dead's guitarist and singer Bob Weir's song *The Other One*. The lyrics in the second verse state: *the bus come by and I got on, that's when it all began; there was cowboy Neil (Cassady) at the wheel, the bus to never ever land.*

It was my first Grateful Dead show. I found out quickly why it was called a show and not a concert. You either love them or don't. There's usually no in between. I don't think anyone has ever gotten off the bus. It's a conscious decision, but rarely does someone experience the Dead, then disembark. If you get it, you get it forever. I consider my first Grateful Dead concert, on this night, to be my official initiation.

A Grateful Dead concert begins in the parking lot with a tradition of controlled chaotic and peaceful mayhem revolving around a designated and centralized location called "Shakedown Street." Named after a song of the Grateful Dead, this "street" is a market of survival for the Deadheads that choose to live on tour and travel with the band. The Deadheads set up shop, along this strip of parking lot, selling whatever they have produced, in clothing, food, jewelry, and memorabilia. The sales finance their voyage to the next town and show. Of course, the street is accompanied by an ongoing soundtrack of kind music and scents in the air. Whether shopping or strolling, Shakedown Street overcomes the individual with a welcoming tradition of truly arriving at the show. The entire parking lot scene is the start to something greater. Harmony, peace and smiles set me off on this night, knowing it would be a good night. It was one I will never forget.

As a rookie follower that night, my friends led me through the parking lot stopping every few minutes to talk to someone new. It was as if they knew half the people in the parking lot. A somber topic of conversation revealed a sense of mourning and a new reality for my new friends, the Deadheads. Less than two months prior, on July 26, 1990, the third keyboardist of the Grateful Dead, Brent Mydland, passed away. My new friends together spoke about their loss, as if a family member passed. Just one and a half months later, as the 1990 Fall Tour recently embarked in newness of lineup, they compared and contrasted the new stage set up of the keyboards and, of course, the new sound of keys and vocals that were replaced by Bruce Hornsby and Vince Welnick. It was new and difficult for the Dead Heads. But I could tell in their passionate words and conversation, they were collectively consoling each other, while embarking on a new tradition of the greatest show on earth.

As we got primed for the show, fungus again became our choice of party favors. The brigade of Deadheads, walking towards The Spectrum, became a parade of chattering, euphoric hippies. The anticipation of the first note played by the band was rising quicker than the degrees in a desert afternoon. It quickly became my personal reality that each person felt an individual and collective spirit towards tonight's festivities. We, as fans, are part of the show. Our only requirement was to bring peace and enthusiasm. Security and ticketing seemed to take forever as the caravan of sight and sound got more crowded and muffled. I'm sure the mushrooms were kicking in and affecting the reality of space, time and sound.

We made our way down to the floor of the Spectrum and we quickly reveled in our seats that were 10 rows from the stage. Each band member commanded his own station on stage. My friends told me that Jerry Garcia would be right in front of me. I waited in anticipation. No band or music yet; but, a carnival like atmosphere consumed me. Whistles, balloons, laughter and hysterics were engulfing The Spectrum.

Two sets of drums overlooked the three oriental rugs that the front bandmates: Phil, Bobby and Jerry stood upon and performed. There was that El Coyote living room experience again. I patted a dozen balloons back into the air during mid-conversation. Each balloon was my contribution to the pregame festivities. I listened to my speaker while watching the balloon converge on another hippie's domain. Conversation bombarded each of my ears. I was hearing two or three conversation simultaneously. Perpetual smiles of anticipatory glory painted the faces of the Deadheads.

This time I was equipped with proper tie-dyed threads and other hippie apparel purchased on Shakedown Street. The fungus roared through my system and was getting the best of me. Last time, it was only the El Coyote and Willie and The Poor Boys. This time I had arrived and it was my official maiden voyage of the Grateful Dead along with 18,000 hippies consuming every spirited inch of the Philadelphia Spectrum.

I looked up, yet again, at my tall "sponsored brother" of the Grateful Dead and he knew right away that he might be losing me to the paranoia of fungus and the vibrations of the pre-show festivities. I didn't have to say a word. He hugged me saying "hang in their buddy, the show will start soon." He then said: "Every person in this place is looking down and wishing they were in our seats right now." The later words did not aid in helping the paranoia subside. All I heard was that everyone was staring at me. His words, company and hug contained an altruistic and stoic spirit and purpose. I rode that spirit onward.

To combat my hallucinogen paranoia, I constructed a new reality in my heart and mind. I filled my heart with love and connectivity. While my friend was attending his 20th, 30th or 80th show (not sure how many he went to up to that point), tonight's performance was superiorly special for him because it was my first show. His contentment during the concert, was living through my first experience, knowing the joy it would bring me. He would experience my maiden voyage into a world, that today, I still consider to be one of the greatest phenomena of musical and cultural history: The Grateful Dead.

The lights of the Spectrum went down and I never heard a louder roar of happiness and excitement by fans in all my life. No walk off homerun or last second field goal could capture the spirited nature of the lights going down at a Grateful Dead show.

Immediately, the mystery of the first note and the revealing of which song they would open up the show with consumed each Deadhead. It is the mutually shared signature cognition of the individual and collective anticipation. Each Grateful Dead show and set list of songs was unique to that date and town. One might go to 5 or 6 shows in a row and not here a single song repeated.

The roars continued as the band stepped on stage, picked up their instruments and tuned up preparing themselves and their fans for that first note and lift-off. From the lights going down to the first note, I was not sure if it lasted a half a minute to a half hour, but with the fungus consumption I lean towards the later. The front men, Bobby, Phil and Jerry walked from amps to pedals checking and double checking their sounds. There was no check one, two, three, four. Volume increased and decreased. Hearts were beating simultaneously to amplified twangs and percussions being wacked, by Mickey and Bill, the drummers. Musical confusion and preparedness filled the air in harmony. Hints of songs excited the fans. I stood there wondering what the fuck is going on here.

When nothing becomes something during the band's pre-tune up, revealing the first note/song of a Grateful Dead show, it is as if all time stops and gold has been struck after decades of searching for the treasure. Some of my first note/song Grateful Dead experiences found me dancing to the tune up and then realizing 3 minutes later that the song had actually started. I realized that I was dancing the same way to a song as I was to the tuning session. Vibrations are real and contagious. It appeared that nothing is always something at a Grateful Dead concert; if you let it.

Tonight, was not that case, as my first note of sight and sound was a D minor chord that blew my mind. My life would be changed forever. The first chord/note of the song, *Shakedown Street* is a D minor chord. While a minor chord is traditionally regarded and felt as a sad chord, this collection of notes in a chord to open up this song, along with the ligh simultaneously coming up, became my baptism into a world that I never leave, even in sobriety.

As I type this chapter, the glory of technology and You by the efforts of my new online Deadhead friend, w recently posted the actual concert in its entirety. Presently, I am watching and listening to my first Grateful Dead show from 28 years ago. That baptism (the opening song Shakedown Street) lasted 14 minutes and has sustained itself for my lifetime. Ironically, later that night, in the second set, the band also performed "The Other One" and the bus came by and I got on. I've never gotten off. Next stop is the next show. I'm in!

The glaring and permanent experience of that night is too long to write. I hope I've done it justice to my family of Deadheads reading this book. I've been to shows high and sober. I've experienced community and exhilaration at all of the shows I've attended. It is a life changing experience at each show.

I truly believe that the Grateful Dead music and their fans encompass and distribute a collective harmonious asset to this world. Brought together by music, the ripple of our movement is in peace and kindness towards everyone. No one is isolated, discriminated or burdened by this assemblage of people. Acceptance and harmony are the touchstone of this collective musical reality that will never end.

Many people stigmatize the deadheads and community of the Grateful Dead. To those people, I remind them that in our United States government, Catholic Church and practically every organization that exists today; there are always some individuals that create toxicity. No room for that in my book or life. Those individuals should not steal away the mission and goodness created by the masses. The collective should always outweigh the individual.

On that unforgettable night, September 10, 1990, as I danced 100 feet/ 10 rows away from Jerry Garcia, with 18,000 other people, each of them becoming my dance partner, I found myself following and evaluating the lights and music working in coordination. Light shows are an artform. Being in the 10th row, the lights and fungus mutually contributed to my _____ I was swathed by the light show. The music moved and the _____ of my being. Whether real or a personally _____ rney that night, I followed the red and blue _____ with the music. At times, they hovered over _____ ts created a thermostatic change in my core _____ my sweat output. The blue lights gave me a euphoric air conditioner relief from the reds. Each colored light had its own mission. It appeared mutual to our entire section of concert attendees.

In the first song I ever wrote, *Two Claps of Thunder*, my bridge lyrics contain a line etching that life changing experience of touring with the Grateful Dead on my soul:

"Why can't I go home, just for one night
I'm following the blues and reds, from The Grateful Dead
And I'm counting my blessings and bidding my goodbyes
To the world that I leave behind"

Copywrite 2005 by Mike Brill "Two Claps of Thunder"

I am cautious to look into the past and share about my Grateful Dead experiences. I embrace the individual experiences, while realizing I let it be a contribution to my addiction progression and eventual demise. In sharing this experience, I do not mean to glorify drug use.

I do not use the word regret nor do I live in it. Regret is a useless and unproductive state of mind. The world itself imprisons me.

When I got sober, people told me I would become happy, joyous and free. Happy and joyous I understood by witnessing other people's smile and share about their happiness. The reality goal of freedom I did not fully comprehend. As sobriety continued and became more solidified, I came to the realization that the freedom from sobriety is being able to go and do anything I want to do as a responsible sober human being. I did not get sober to exclude one of my greatest healing passions in my life: music, especially the music of the Grateful Dead.

Today, I still attend Grateful Dead type concerts. I attend as a person living in long term recovery and a *Warf Rat* who is responsible for his life and sobriety. I attend with a freedom, rooted in a personal commitment to firm spiritual and recovery practices. *Warf Rat* is a song by the Grateful Dead that contains powerful lyrics:

But I'll get back on my feet again someday, the
good Lord willin', if He says I may.

*I know that the life I'm livin's no good, I'll get
a new start, live the life I should*

Copywrite: Grateful Dead 1971

At festivals and concerts, *The Warf Rats* are a support organization of recovering, concert attending Dead Heads that choose to live alcohol and drug free. The Warf Rats set up a booth onsite at concerts and festivals, with yellow balloons signifying their presence and mission for ongoing support to anyone in recovery attending the concert. At set break, a recovery meeting takes place. Throughout the concert, fans in recovery wear yellow stickers that read: One Show at a Time. At any point of the concert, I am able to talk to these people or walk to the booth for recovery support.

Brill Dancing to the music of the Grateful Dead

CHAPTER 6

We Will Survive

Over the next five years of my life, I saw the Grateful Dead with Jerry Garcia about 40 times. Unfortunately, in one of my many relocations, I lost my ticket stubs and cannot recollect the exact number of shows. I added 2 – one hundred cassette holders to my collection, with the recent additions containing decorated cassette tapes, commemorating live Grateful Dead shows. Live recordings became the legal, cherished commodity of Deadheads to assist in aiding the music to literally never stop. Only one band allows their shows to be recorded by fans. No record company or contract could stop the Grateful Dead from providing this cherished and luxurious musical memory to their fans. The tradition of collecting and keeping mementos became even more sacred and cherished when our community lost their beloved leader, Jerry Garcia.

On August 9, 1995, while working at a law firm, in Center City Philadelphia, one of my many jobs I held shortly during my 20's and progression of addiction, I returned from an internal mail run. My coworker shared with me that Jerry Garcia died. After a blurry short denial, I saw in his genuine hippie heart that he was serious; as it became apparent through my recognition of his own realized grief and loss. He understood the Grateful Dead and its spirit. We established that in our working environment. A few of the bike messengers, stationed in the other room, in their innocent ignorance, verbalized some taunting and joking of my traumatic loss. I retreated quickly, without response to their obvious obliteration of what this man meant to me and countless others. I ran down one floor, skipping two or three steps at a time, into a corner men's room, locked the stall door and just cried.

It was at that point I came to realize what people meant when they asked where you were when JFK was shot and killed. This generational question conceptualizes and brings forth an extreme parameter of negative timely experience and its level of personal effect. The question solidifies history.

I left work early that afternoon, and I cried all the way home on the El train through Philadelphia and back home to my apartment in Frankford. I walked into my apartment and immediately put on Jerry's song *Days Between*. I listened to that song over a hundred times throughout the sad duration of the next 24 hours.

On that somber day, during the first live recorded delivery of my favorite slow song of the Dead, sung by Jerry Garcia, *Days Between*, I walked over to my voicemail recorder and played the only message beeping. It was my mother's voice. Without hesitation, my mother verbalized her sincere condolences to me on losing Jerry Garcia. "I know what he meant to you and I'm so sorry for your loss, Michael" she stated. She used my full first name, which usually only meant I was in trouble. This time, she was an empathetic mother consoling her youngest child in his bereavement. While shocked to hear this sympathy from my mother, my tears quadrupled, realizing her altruistic love, that only a mother could display.

My mother experienced my adopted progression of a chaotic lifestyle through my active tenure as a Grateful Dead fan. My motivations and behaviors, during those previous five years touring with the Dead, were unpredictable and precarious. The loss of school and jobs being a tiresome experience for my mother (and father). I got caught up and was in the birthing and nurturing of my disease of addiction. I normalized it again by thinking this is what I'm supposed to be doing in my 20's. I will survive.

In the later afternoon, after countless tears and renditions of *Days Between*, my upstairs neighbor and lifelong friend came home from work. We had been friends since the second grade, when I asked him to come over after school, to play hockey. He lived in my huge Catholic parish, but on the other side of "town." It wasn't the bad part of town, simply far away. We became friends that day and the bond has only gotten stronger with time. He played football and I played soccer and golf. I went away to school and he worked for his dad's carpet company, eventually spurring off into his own business. We have gone our separate ways but never miss a beat when we are together. Early in my sobriety, he asked me to play music for his beautiful wedding. Later in my life, I asked him to be in my wedding. Our friendship has lasted and our glue became the Grateful Dead and Jerry Garcia.

On that sad day, out loss bonded us tighter. He lived upstairs in the duplex. His front door was in the driveway, while my front door was in the back yard. Today, he bypassed his front door. He walked in my door, through my kitchen and into my living room. With the music blaring, we did not say a word to each other. We simply hugged. Two men hugging and crying because on that day we were collectively lost as our muse to the greatest musical experiences of our lives left this world without warning. My friend and I continue to share the live music experience in whatever capacity The Grateful Dead music is provided. We will get by.

CHAPTER 7

Let There Be Songs
To Fill The Air

I took guitar lessons at age 11. After a year of lessons, since I wasn't John Lennon by that time, I quit. A long, drunken, high night at one of my college's fraternities revealed my talent still existed.

After a huge bong hit, I picked up my buddy's guitar and began playing The Beatles' song *Blackbird*. The room went silent. It had been almost 11 years since I touched a guitar and the song rolled out of me, like I'd rehearsed it that afternoon. The next day, in a blurry hangover, I called my Mom and asked for a guitar that Christmas. Since receiving that gift, I have taught myself and have been performing professionally for the past 27 years. The guitar and music have been a huge part of my healing and spirituality. But it wasn't always like that. Intentions and motivations are truly major ingredients to output.

After my first failure at college, I dropped out and wandered. I dwelled up in the Poconos, simply existing and touring with the Grateful Dead. Returning to home, family and Philadelphia with my tail between my legs, I met a guy from the neighborhood. He played the guitar and we spent many nights down by the Delaware River freely jamming and learning tunes together. He drove an amazing classic convertible car. My new friend was definitely appealing to the girls. The river, guitars and a classic car created a nice opportunity to feel cool and meet the ladies. I simply tagged along. Eventually, bored with just river jam sessions soothing our souls, we were ready for live performances. We adopted my older brother to sing some vocals and my first band *Lemuel Lo'* was born.

Lemuel Lo' is a character from one of my favorite books, *Weaveworld*, written by Clive Barker. In the book, during a secret excursion into the world woven into a rug, like only Clive Barker could create, the lead character comes across an amphitheater where Lemuel Lo' is conducting, as an MC, to sort of an open mic vibe. Lemuel Lo' was creating and encouraging a space of openly sharing gifts of the arts. As the lead character secretly crept around the forum of the arts, he was called out by Lo'. Lemuel Lo' verbally referred to this main character's late father's gifts of the arts in order to encourage him to share his own. Lemuel Lo's character was described as a larger, white bearded man. I attached his identity to Jerry Garcia.

After a few official Lemuel Lo' practices in my brother's duplex basement, that I christened "The Underground Treefort," we rented a PA system and started performing in local bars. This began a 27-year career, passion and gift of performing music. Daddy O's, Fathead's, Mugshots, Rauchut's, Coaches or whatever alcohol establishment that would host us became our tour destinations. Free alcohol became my primary motivation in performing live music.

My first personal and professional attempt in keeping the music that I love alive was in my next band, *Sizzlecat Sunshine*. This was my first venture into the electric music world. It surely wasn't advertised or embraced as much as Bob Dylan's transition to the electric sound. However, adding drums, amps and electric guitar was a new world to me. My brother and I found a great guy; singer and guitarist. He and his girlfriend transplanted to Philadelphia, after college. A lifelong friend joined us on the drums. Friends and the live music scene brought us together and I'm forever grateful for their presence in my life and music. We were a 4-piece jam band performing covers of the Grateful Dead and other influential artists from that era. In a creative and unique way, we threw in surprise cover songs. Performing The Cure's, *Just like Heaven*, with a reggae strum was one of those exclusive creations.

Along with our own souls, we kept people happy with our interpretive vibrations of the music that we all loved. It was perfect timing. We were performing Grateful Dead music during the dark time of losing Jerry

Garcia. We did our best to keep the light lit and soothe hippies in their time of mourning.

I continued my musical sharing of this music in bands such as: Acoustic Junction and Project J.A.M. I met my new musical partner at a party and immediately we got along. I joined him on guitar and he taught me the chords to Neil Young's song, *Pocahontas*. Our vocal harmonies melted my socks and truly deserved further musical exploration. We added a friend to the congas and our people followed us providing more soothing continuance of the Grateful Dead music.

A gift of early sobriety came when my brother organized an Irish Cultural Event in the Lehigh Valley. He asked me and my brothers to get together and perform some Irish music for the festivities. Our band, *The Sons of Dot*, was born. Me and my three older brothers practiced and learned Irish music to perform. For a few years, especially around St. Patrick's Day, we ended up playing many shows. It was a time where music, family and my parent's legacy, collectively became a prevalent force in my new sober life.

Brill with his brothers performing in their band The Sons of Dot

My addictions spiraled during the prior bands. Opportunity and convenience at live shows combined for a toxic reality. My addiction progression was the primary root of problems and demise of all my bands. With alcohol and drugs being my motivation for performing music, the music suffered. I just couldn't see I was the problem. Sex, Drugs and Alcohol became my normalization mantra. I thought, isn't this what all musicians do? Each night, an abundance of drugs and alcohol polluted my system. Eventually, I destroyed every quality intimate relationship. Soon as I was the only company I could maintain (barely), I disregarded sex from my story, as it got in the way of my partying.

It got to the point that at the beginning of performances my hands shook so much that I could not strum a chord or hold down the strings. I frequently ran off stage to consume multiple shots of liquor, to steady myself, in order to perform. As the night and performance progressed, it only got uglier. Each first practice, after weekend gigs, initiated a band dialogue pertaining to my drunken performance and lack of professionalism.

During the downfall of these great bands, my era of "tears of a clown" began. The make-up and façade blossomed when I lost my parents to cancer, within 8 months of each other.

Chapter 8

The Tears Of A Clown

Now if there's a smile on my face, It's only there trying to fool the public
But when it comes down to fooling you, Now that's quite a different subject
But don't let my glad expression, give you the wrong impression
Really I'm sad, oh I'm sadder than sad

In these lyrics of *Tears of a Clown* by Smokey Robinson "Fooling you" refers to a self-conversation in the mirror. The clown is revealing his truest level of low self-esteem, while realizing the smiles and make up, along with everything good that encapsulates being a clown, is truly a façade. Generally, the mission of a clown is to ignite smiles and laughter from their audience, especially in children. However, in this song, the human clown, is coming to the harshest realization of being unhappy and sad - a clown's crossroad of personal truth.

As I was living in a lie, I put forth exhaustive efforts to ultimately believe the lie, myself. My false beliefs were maintained to portray a "truth" to others. Excepting a lie as a truth, especially over time, brings forth dire consequences to one's measure of reality and self-esteem. A literal fairytale is born and nurtured. For me, through lies, the abnormal became normal.

Over the years, used car salesmen have gotten a reputation for their strategy of selling a lemon(car); while consciously knowing that the car would not last on the road over 1,000 miles or even to the first traffic light. The technological advancement of online car purchasing services, such as Carfax, was a direct response to this hideous sales tactic. What sort of services do we have for individual humans telling themselves lies, false truths? A liar ignores his conscious reality. Subconsciously, over time, lies covering lies becomes crippling and debilitating.

In December of 1995, while living in the Frankford section of Northeast Philadelphia, I received a phone call from my mother. She shared that my father had been diagnosed with cancer. I was 25 years old. This news came as my world of independent living was crumbling around me and my addictions were roaring. From this phone call, although being sad, I felt a burst of positive motivation. In my mind, I would become the household's Florence Nightingale to assist in the healing and supporting of my parents. My plan was to move back home and help my mother take care of my father. I wanted to become that son. I had a plan and all I could see was goodness coming out of the decision to move back home. I was ignoring my main problem- Me.

Core values in the form of great parents and family traditions, all within me, were ignored and lost. But still existed somewhere. I saw this as an opportunity to embark on something good in my life, despite it being born out of a challenging hardship, my father's cancer. I was attempting to turn my life around by showing others I could be an asset in my parent's lives. I felt this would be a behavioral modification witnessed by others that would set my life on a healthy pathway. My intention was created to show others in the external world, while still not giving the proper attention to my own demons in my internal world.

At the time, I was behind on my rent and all financial responsibilities, as I walked away from my job at the law firm. I just didn't show up to work to avoid being fired. Everything was always on my terms. I had to no other job or opportunity waiting for me. I put forth efforts to collect unemployment and be lazy. In my freezer laid endless hits of LCD. I was doing acid at least 2 times a week, frequently by myself. I was drinking every day of the week. If my eyes were open and I was vertical, I was drinking alcohol. Cocaine was never refused either. Two, three or four substances at a time was not uncommon.

The opportunity of helping my parents did not automatically create Tabula Rasa, a blank slate, in my world. My slate was filled with increasing debilitating issues surrounding my personal lifestyle and addictions. Now, my motivation, opportunity and plan of helping my mother and father, in their time of need, whether authentic in intention or not, simply was just that: a cognitive plan. At that time in my life, I was unable to help myself, but I sold myself and others on my capabilities to become an asset in another's healing. I moved back home and with me I brought my addictions and chaos.

Back living in my parent's home, my drinking and drug use continued, even heightening more prominently, after getting a waitering job at a local bar/restaurant. The tradition of the hospitality business is to work hard for tips and party accordingly. At least, that is what it became for me. One shift led to a 2-day party for me. At the beginning of each shift, I was penniless.

At the time, I told people in grandiose fashion, that I moved back home to help my mother take care of my father who had cancer. I remember soaking in the way people looked at me and complimented me on my "selfless" efforts and decision. I sold my story of façade to anyone that would listen. Deep down, existing at my core, I knew that is what healthy Mike Brill would do for his parents. At this time, it was the furthest from the reality. Meanwhile, I was missing days at a time and my parents added frontline worry to their daily agenda, wondering where I was and if was still alive. I was MIA, only returning home to shower, change, check in than get to my cash paying job that allowed my party to continue daily. I was living out my internal "lemon." The curtain hiding the truth was being pulled back slowly with each poor decision I made. The truth was surfacing. All my energy was equally distributed between my "selfless" tale of helping my parents and staying drunk.

In the fall of 1996, at age 26, as my addictions roared forward, my mother's heath began to decline. I ignored all signs. I wouldn't admit Mom was sick, as Dad was dying. Those times were foggy, but eventually I heard my worst nightmare, in my mother's diagnosis of Pancreatic Cancer.

In desperation, one of my outward displays of positive life efforts to please my external world, (namely my parents), was the first of my many returns to college in 1996. I enrolled in a summer course at LaSalle University, portraying concrete external efforts in change to my loved ones. Still, no attention or efforts of internal change was taking place in my life. A personal internal process of that magnitude would have taken honest accountability and responsibility. I was not ready for those efforts in change.

My drink of choice that summer was Non-Alcohol (NA) Busch Beer. The can looked exactly like the regular alcohol selection with a tiny red NA on the can. I would buy a six pack of non-alcohol and a case of alcohol Busch cans and drink them accordingly, depending on my company. I was putting more make up on this clown's face with every purchase and drink.

During one of my mother's hospital stays, I was at home and received a delivery of medical supplies to our house. This was in preparation for my brother Joe's wedding on the following weekend. This was an event my mother would not miss and her medical team did everything to help make her wedding attendance a reality.

One afternoon, on my way to my night class, I stopped by to see my mom in the hospital. She looked great and it was a very special moment for me. She was hopeful for me and was happy with my return to school, despite my deviant selective drinking habits. She believed I was off the booze. Or so I thought and believed. I got up to leave her hospital room to attend school and we embraced and we each said: "I love you." She told me that she was proud of me. Not knowing, at the time, that cherished hospital visit, a gift we provided each other, was the last time I spoke to my mother.

I came home to my parent's home that night, after school, to an empty house. In those days, there were no cell phones, and I went upstairs to check the answering machine. A single flashing red light lit my parent's dark bedroom, announcing a message. To this day, I don't remember who from my family left the message, but the voice told me mom fell after I left the hospital and she had a turn for the worse. A stressed tone of voice pleaded that I should come to the hospital immediately.

Around 10:30pm, I was walking through the parking lot, towards the entrance of the hospital, and saw my uncle walking in with coffees in tow. He said: "Michael, brace yourself, it's not good." After embracing family members, I walked into my mother's room and she laid there with tubes running everywhere. One tube, being in her mouth, sustaining her breaths of life. My tears dropped with every beep and whistle of the medical machines. The smiling, happy, glowing woman I had left 5 hours prior, when we verbalized our love for each other, was now motionless, eyes closed and fighting for her life.

Our family camped out at the hospital, coming to the sad realization that my brother's wedding would go on without Mom. I remember only a few things from that day, as NA beer was no longer on my menu. My main thoughts and emotions consuming me that day, were manifested in how sad I was for my brother on his supposedly happy wedding day.

In our little rowhome in Northeast Philadelphia, my brothers, Dad and I got ready, dressing in our tuxes and singing to the Irish Music blaring from the stereo. Our local phenomenal Irish Band: *Blackthorn*, filled our Cottage Street house. Irish music is fascinatingly powerful. It can be the distractor or stimulator of raw emotions by the listener, especially if Irish. This day was brother Joe's and my father led the directive and goal of making this a memorable day, despite our mother's condition and approaching demise. As we drank, danced and dressed, during Terence Winch's song *When New York Was Irish*, our friend, the founding member, guitarist and singer from *Blackthorn* powerfully belted out his version and sang the lyrics:

> *They were ever so happy, they were ever so sad*
> *To grow old in the new land, through good times and bad*
> *All the parties and the weddings, the ceilis, and the wakes*
> *When New York was Irish full of joy and heartache*

Copyright: 1987 Terrance Winch

On this grand day, the Brill brothers loudly sang right along with their friend. While this song and specific lyrics, during this time in my family's trauma, should cause us to breakdown, I remember our patriarchal leader, Dad, coming into our bedrooms to distract his sons' tears from falling. He diverted us with Irish language trivia and asked us about the lyric/ word, *ceili*. Dad asked proudly, "Do you guys even know what a *ceili* is?" We looked at each other, all hoping one of us could come up with the answer for dad. My father's kind and pure Irish soul proceeded to give us primary clues. He shared with his sons that we have been a part of *ceilis* and witnessed them our whole lives. He interjected, that we just never knew what it was called, within the Irish tradition. He reflected aloud, in proud storytelling fashion, of the past times when he would lead the singing around the dining room table, to all hours of the morning, long after us kids were sleeping in bed. This happened every time my parents hosted or attended a party. A *ceili* is defined as a social event or gathering that involves friendship, family, singing, dancing and storytelling.

On that morning of the wedding, with his appropriately timed Irish trivia, my dad provided a life-long nugget of Irish distraction for his boys to embrace. But I think, most of all, at that moment, with his best friend and soul mate, Dotty/Mom, laying in a hospital bed on a breathing tube, Dad soothed his own soul and terminated his own tears, with a personal reflection and story to his sons of the happiest memories that he and Mom shared. Fair play, Dad....fair play!

To begin the wedding ceremony, my brother and I walked our father down the long aisle at St. Bartholomew's Church. My parents sent four boys to that school and dedicated their entire lives to the church and parish. Immediately, the wedding appeared to adopt a funeral like atmosphere. Tears flowed from every eye on both the groom and bride's sides of the church. My mother was missing and everyone knew why she wasn't proudly marching down the aisle with her husband. We tried to put on our game faces for our brother. However, the tears of others ignited our own fears and tears. Dad and his two youngest sons strolled down the aisle and smiled tearfully.

After the ceremony and pictures, on our way to the reception, our wedding party stopped off at Jean's Hospital to visit our mother. I'm not sure what medical technology was used on my mother before our arrival, but the outcome gave me a reality and picture of my mother that makes me shudder to this day. After days of having a breathing tube in and no response from Mom, we walked into her hospital room and Mom was propped up with her eyes opened. It was a Lazarus moment for me. While momentous at the time of this occasion, it also provided me with a false hope that Mom was going to be alright and would live.

We filled the room with tears, seeing Mom with her eyes opened, but unable to talk. I think I remember tears in her eyes, as her eyes moved back and forth as her son walked in with his new bride. I'm not sure how long we stayed because we had a reception to attend. The reception must go on. We danced and celebrated for our brother.

The next day, with bloodshot eyes and a crippling hangover, I returned to the hospital on Sunday with my family. My brother had cancelled his honeymoon. His first two days of marriage would be witnessing the death of his mother. Scores of people came to visit Mom that day. Each of us took our own personal time in Mom's room to reflect, pray, beg, sing or do nothing but remain numb. On my last solo late-night visits to Mom, as the calendar announced November 11, 1996, I sat with her and chose to write a song. I wrote my song: *The World That Should Have Been*

Days are darker while they're long, words slip as though they're wrong
And you slip, as you crawl away
Words you sit they float on by, words you sit and you wonder why,
Can you help me, can you help me find another way

And you dream of the world that should have been
Wondering why it turned out this way
But the dream it is gone
Now there's nothing left to do, but carry the weight

Simple passages last for now, without words from you last thought
Could you help me, could you help me see another day?
Comprehension is understanding. And seeing is believing
Can you help me; Could you help me see another way

And you dream of the world that should have been
Wondering why it turned out this way
But the dream it is gone
Now there's nothing left to do, but carry the weight

Note: Later in my life, as I was slowly dying, with my addictions becoming apparent and real to all around me, my friend, born out of his concern for my well-being and hope that I would come through my addiction, wrote this last verse. I felt it was right on point, consistent with my "tears of a clown" mantra and added it to this song of homage and hope on the saddest day of my life. The 3rd verse:

50

My mask is on right now, to hide from the unsuspecting friends
That would like to save my life
Troubled in this world of mine, I find it hard to read between the lines
But I'll stand head up high

And you dream of the world that should have been
Wondering why it turned out this way
But the dream it is gone
And there's nothing left to do, but carry the weight

Copywrite 2019 Mike Brill *"The World That Should Have Been"*

Hours later, after my time with Mom, on November 11, 1996, my mother's hospital room was filled with people she loved and cherished. We prayed and encouraged her to stop fighting. She died fighting.

I remember her last breath. If death can be horrible and beautiful simultaneously, my mother's passing fulfilled that oxymoron. Moments after her soul left that room, my lyrics hit the bottom of the trashcan. The world that should have been, wasn't to be; as my anger, sadness and traumatic loss consumed me. I was content in letting go of my creation that I generated with Mom earlier during my last solitary moments, saying my goodbye to her. Days, weeks, or months later, I'm not sure when, my brother handed me crumpled up pieces of paper. It was the lyrics I tossed away, that I wrote with Mom.

The song lives with me today, containing so many meanings. Mostly, it reminds me that I had those moments with my mom in her final hours. It stands as a lesson in not regretting things in the past and to make the world or accept it exactly as it should be. I have been privileged to share it with so many musicians and fans over the years. A live version of it exists on www.spinningstraw.net/music

The Irish wake for my mother that occurred over the next week kept our house filled with family, friends and alcohol. The grieving oxymoronic reality of tears and laughter passed from one person to the other. On the day after my mom's burial, I was out back of our house with my dad. A newer neighbor, across the back alley, verbalized his condolences again to dad and me. He said to dad that he felt like he was at a royal funeral, referring to the turnout of people and wait time to console the Brill boys and their father in their time of grieving. I often wondered how Dad even survived while diagnosed with his own cancer, battling his own war and then losing his best friend within 5 weeks of Mom's diagnosis.

I continued to live with Dad; while spiraling into the abyss of untreated addictions and trauma. My addiction mutually clouded and exasperated the death trauma in my life. No release was in sight. I had only one coping strategy of healing and it was in alcohol and drugs. I tried to put on my happy face and reveal to everyone that *everything is O.K.*

My brothers came up with the idea to get my Dad to travel to Ireland, the land he loved yet never experienced firsthand. Mom's fear of airplane travel kept such a trip off the option table. As two of my brothers were planning this trip, Dad was sure to communicate his concern of my alcoholic condition and proceeded to take care of all of my present financial debt and other concrete concerns, so that I may join them on this Brill men voyage to the Emerald Isle. My brother told me later in life, that Dad communicated to him that I was going to be a huge concern and verbalized that I was an alcoholic.

As my brothers' spearheading of this trip of a lifetime proceeded, the day came when Dad, through feedback from his doctors, eventually came to the sad realization and verbalized to us that his declining health would not allow him to make the trek to Ireland. As if we needed another sad Irish tale to tell, we postponed the trip and focused on Dad's healing and eventual declining health.

Dad's stomach became a feeding tube and his favorite recliner eventually becoming a hospital bed. Along with other extended family members, we took shifts taking care of Dad. We fed him cans of Ensure mixed with grounded up prescription medicine. Although the family home care efforts embarrassed him, I think our company, during his decline, sustained Dad the most.

A horrific memory, which still haunts me today, occurred during one of my turns in taking care of Dad. It is wreckage of my past that can only be managed through spiritual principles. I had the morning shift. The night before, after a shift at the restaurant, I took my tips to the bar and eventually I don't know where I ended up or how I got home. I don't even remember what family member I relieved from taking care of Dad.

In my parent's row home, they had refinished the basement many years prior. I believe it was to accommodate their growing boys and friends. Also, it equally enhanced my parent's Irish hospitality capabilities. The basement contained a pull-out couch, TV and of course tons of records with an updated stereo system. Our basement and house itself were filled with music any time someone was home. It is truly where my love of music was born.

The new section of the basement, where our garage once existed, was a dart board, with a homemade paneling case constructed by Dad. A second bathroom resided and in a row home in Northeast Philadelphia was a rare find. It benefited the six of us; as well as the many guests who frequented the basement addition.

To the left of the dart board was the homemade bar, Joe Brill's Bar. It was Dad's premier creation, complete with an ice container saying Brill's Bar. The back of the bar was surrounded by mirrors, lights and shelves with all types of bottles of liquor proudly displayed. Under the brown table top bar were two more shelves stocked with booze, mixers and tools of the bartender trade. Dad would not be without someone's specific drink ingredients if they were stepping up to his bar in his house. If you were with Dad at his bar only once, he remembered your drink and would not be without its ingredients. The grand ingredient of Dad's bar was a beer meister. It was never without a ¼ barrel of beer. In my childhood, Schmidts beer, the Philadelphia home brewery, poured from its tap. I forget what happened or what brand was declared after Schmidts Brewery closed down in Philadelphia.

At that point of my drinking, I did not discriminate brands of alcohol. My alcoholic consumption policy was quantity over quality. All I remember is that the brand keg had to have a prong connection, not a ball connector. Important information for my turns to host the keg parties at Dad's bar. The backroom of our basement contained a washer, dryer, refrigerator, independent pantry closet, wall phone and plenty of shelves for storage. Our basement was truly an accessed and enjoyed addition to our home, adding to the honing and mastery of our Irish hospitality skills.

I don't remember much of that dreaded, drunken morning. I returned home, the next morning, after work and partying. That was the extent of my fulfilled responsibility. The permanent memory that lingers and stings is laying on the couch and being awakened with fists, slaps and yelling. I received a justified pounding coupled with verbal commands to "get up and get the fuck out of this house – Go…JUST GO – WE'RE DONE WITH YOU!"

Earlier that morning, during my comatose state of existence in the basement, my father called one of my brothers to say I was not responding or taking my responsibility in feeding and caring for his life and health needs. My father, with a feeding tube in his stomach, crawled through the living room, dining room, and across the linoleum kitchen floor. He pulled and dragged himself down an entire flight of steps to his magnificent basement. As he crawled across the floor, he reached for his youngest son, passed out on the couch. Reaching up from the floor he yelled and shook me to wake me up. There was no response from me. Dad needed to be fed and medicated. His last born and caretaker was fucked up, passed out cold. In my father's dire time of need, he didn't know if I was dead or alive.

After coming too, receiving the justifiable beating and hearing this story, for once, I didn't argue one bit. I was wrong and walked away silently out the door and down the street on foot. At the time, I was permitted to use Dad's car for travel. Not anymore! Now, I had a few more reasons to drink and party. That's just what an alcoholic and addict does best.

To this day, I don't know the time frame or where I existed for the next weeks. All my "lesses" were coming true: jobless, penniless, motherless and now hopelessness shadowing every one of my steps. These realities, in the form of personal justifications, were fueling every drink and drug I consumed. I existed by still selling my tears of a clown sales pitch providing everyone with happy go lucky Mike Brill.

Concern was breathed upon me by people who were troubled and concerned for my well-being. I would return to the same bar from the night before with cuts, bruises, scabs or fresh blood from staggering falls that occurred after closing the same bar, the night before. Bar owner and true friend sadly and reluctantly asked me to leave my cherished Stevenson's Place. He had too. I was a mess, even making a mockery of the live entertainment performing in the bar. It was so sad.

Stevenson's Place and its owner and bartender, my friend, hosted live music and my music for many years. It was a mecca of sharing the arts, seldomly found in NE Philadelphia. I met some of the greatest musicians, who I call friends today. As I became an embarrassment in my drunken ways, the sad outcomes simply became another justification to drink. The frequent truth, more often than not, is that I would return to a bar the next night; not knowing I was drinking there the night prior. Blackouts became frequent.

At 27 years old, the Summer of 1997 was upon me and again I rationalized that sleeping anywhere wasn't that bad. Pending my condition, sympathetic friends would sometimes offer couches in my time of need. I slept anywhere, refusing to admit I was homeless.

After a long night of drinking, on a very early, steamy July morning, I woke up on the floor in my cousin's apartment. I stunk and was sweating profusely. At that time in our lives, my cousin and I had similar interests in the enjoyment of consuming large quantities of beer. This time, I wasn't awakened with punches. Rather, it was the look and a tone of voice of my cousin revealing sheer concern. He told me that my brother called and said that I needed to immediately get up to the house. Dad is not doing well.

My brothers found me. I guess through the grapevines of Northeast Philadelphia it's not difficult to find out about people. It's not a gossip trait. Rather, it appears everyone knows everyone. Seven degrees of Northeast Philadelphians is alive and driven by being known by your parish or playground where you played sports, chased girls, hung out and eventually drank alcohol.

I rolled over and eventually got myself up off the floor. I was guided and motivated by strong convincing encouragement from my cousin. Alcohol wanted me to roll over. Family won the debate. Shame, guilt and remorse, not to mention the 95-degree July morning, made my 7-minute walk home feel like an intercontinental crusade. I wanted a drink. Even with the degree of severity of this morning phone call from my brother; the failing condition of my father and the ramifications of my previous decisions and behaviors, my solitary thought and hope was that I could get to that beer miester in the basement for a cold one. I staggered down my beloved Cottage Street.

Stepping out of an alley or driveway as we called them, I turned down the treeless block towards the house I grew up in. It felt like years, not weeks, since I'd been there. Our rowhome was a ¼ of the way down the block. We use to have one tree outside our house and one across the street.

In full summer bloom, the trees distracted our across-the-street wiffle ball games. The batter was across the street and the pitcher in front of my house. We had designated boundaries declaring the hit: single, double, triple and hitting the house being a homerun. If the wiffle-ball went into our trees and caught, it was an out. Otherwise, a foul ball was declared. Over twenty years of wiffle ball games occurred on our street. No one was hit by a car.

As I approached the house, I slid by the old stone wall, dragging my fingers along the frazzled cement. Different cement formations shot upward from the top of the wall. It was a decorative addition to the wall, that gave rise to many dangerous balancing games. As kids, we would walk across them, balancing and often times racing each other, to see who could do it faster. While the one side contained a plush garden and lawn, the other side revealed a 4 foot drop to the concrete sidewalk below. I came to the end of the wall and turned up the first flight of six cement steps.

To my left, was the two-teared lawn, which I cut many times while growing up; a chore passed down from brother to brother. The lawn was connected to our neighbor's lawn and stood as the playing field for amazing childhood football games; such as, slow mo(tion) football or goal line de(fense), where one kid battled the others to make it through the human wall, at all costs, descending onto the sidewalk declaring a TD in our cement end zone. Snow days were the best.

My feet than carried me up the two midway steps, declaring my halfway ascent point of reaching the front door. I reached the top tier of the lawn, which kissed a cement patio. As I continued my path towards the next set of steps, I paused and could envision my mom standing there, with the hose in hand, watering her beloved rose bushes, garden and lawn. The patio often held a summer setting of furniture and table, set up for relaxing, admiration and an opportunity of flagging down a car or walker to bring them into the warm house for some hospitality. As a child, the patio hosted my playpen. One day, while my brother and his friend were playing with their toy soldiers while Mom was inside taking care of the house, I almost died. In the old days, playpens were mesh. I fell and my hat's button got stuck in the mesh. In my infancy, I hung turning blue, breathless and close to lifeless. My brother saved my life. He called for my Mom and unlatched my hat.

The last 6 cement steps, guided by a white painted iron railing, leading up to the door, was the spot where I learned how to play my guitar. I would sit out there and play for myself and anyone that would listen. My friend who lived across street, still credits me with his passion for music and becoming a guitarist. He was inspired by me and has become an inspiration for me in so many ways.

Today, I wasn't inspiring, rather I was barely existing.

On the final step, I breathed in the humid summer air, closed my eyes and reached for the white, steel storm door handle. Since it was summer and the family were expecting me, the inside door, with its Irish Claddagh door knocker hung perfectly in the middle, was already ajar.

I walked in the door of our rowhome that puts your directly into the living room. Inside the door directly in front of me, the carpeted steps went straight up to the bedrooms and bathroom. Three bedrooms and one bathroom housed six people. It was comfortable, because that's what we had and we made it work. To my left, stood a lamp sitting on top of the glass and brass end-tables. One end table and lamp at each end of the L-shaped white, gray and tan patterned sectional couch surrounded the glass and brass coffee table set in the middle. The 80s décor still not marrying the 1990's.

The living room that saw so many happy people and festive celebrations, now reeked of sickness, with reflections of a lingering hospital aroma. My own stench did not help. On a thirty-degree angle, off to my left, I came eye to eye with my father. Where my father's favorite recliner once resided, now laid my father dying in a hospital bed. He was propped up halfway, looking frail; but still delivered me a warm smile across the room. I don't remember who was in the room with my father at the moment of my entrance, but they quickly dispersed. I took about 8 steps towards my father and sat in an already provided chair. I cried. I held his hand. I heard his words. I cried more.

The house was silent, other than my sniffling and dad's quiet, raspy voice. His cancer was now rampant in his lungs and lymph nodes. My alcoholism and drunkenness did not allow me the verbatim recollection of our conversation. I wished I listened, not just heard him speaking. Drunken recollection only steals from reality. My father told me, on that morning, that if I wanted to, I could do anything that I wanted to, in terms of goals and aspirations. He said that I was more than capable, reminding me that I am good person. Giving it to my straight, he told me I have to get my shit together and make better decisions. And then he said it: *"you're an alcoholic, Mike and until you get a handle on it, more of the same stuff is going to keep happening in your life."*

Three minutes earlier, approaching the front door, I wished I had died in my playpen. After hearing (not listening) my father's words, low self-esteem defeated a dying father's words to his son. I still wanted to die, while wanting my father to live. I cried, apologized and made peace with my father that morning. We cried together and sat silently, holding each other's hand. I just kept saying "I'm so sorry, Dad."

This moment and his words are the treasured gifts of gold that my father provided me that resounds and compounds in my heart and soul each day I stay sober. I did nothing to earn that treasure. But it happened, and I nurture its existence in my soul daily. I am forever grateful and committed to honor that moment. I still say "I'm sorry" every day to my parents.

I remember getting up from my chair and walking around the house; giving my family hugs, kisses and love. I could feel, and rightfully so, their endless concern on my well-being and future. I can only imagine what I looked and smelt like in my appearance that morning.

Avoiding a cold beer at that time of the morning, I went outside with my little neighbors, whose love and concern for Dad surpassed their tender years in age. They knew what was happening and were really going through an emotional harsh reality of death and losing their neighbor. Mom and Dad had a way with kids. Born out of isolating myself from the family and not feeling comfortable inside my family house, I took solace and felt a usefulness in talking and playing with them, if only for our own mutual distraction.

Someone came out the front door and called for me to come back to the house. It was time. I was 27 years old, and after I heard the voice calling me in, I felt like a 7-year-old being called in for dinner. Or least I wished it was that scenario.

Similar to my mother's passing, 8 months prior, we were all present and gathered around the man for his departure from this earth. I often called him Pop Brill. Sons, sisters, aunts, uncles, godchildren, nephews, nieces, cousins and dads two buddies (local priests) from his beloved St. Bartholomew's parish gathered, encouraging and guiding him towards his reunion with Mom and to be home with God. He lived his life for this Catholic faith becoming his personal reality.

I don't remember this occurring through my own tears and traumatic loss; but family members reported that just before Dad's last breath, our living room filled with the scent of roses. My mother went to Little Flower High School and her ongoing patron saint, whom she offered daily reflections, was St. Theresa "The Little Flower of Jesus." This saint is always pictured with a bouquet of roses.

From my family's reported experience of smelling this distinct and beautiful aroma of roses; my mother and father's love for each other; their lifelong Catholic dedication and faith; and my own personal construed belief of death and afterlife; I hold in my heart today that Mom came to Cottage Street, to their home, on that hot July afternoon and met Dad. She was the first to meet him. She was his solitary welcoming committee. Together, they walked into their paradise, they called heaven. They greeted God and live happily ever after.

Mom, Dad and God are now my Higher Powers.

The next 6 ½ years of my life was an ongoing spiral into the abyss of addictions. My two friends allowed me time to live in their homes. I believe I would have died homeless, without their kindness, while planting a kind and hopeful seed in my heart. I would not water those seeds for a while. During that time, if my eyes were open and I was vertical I was using any type of substance. Eventually, the vertical requirement was no longer a requirement on my drinking and using drugs. I could call it a hair of the dog habit; but few hangovers happened; as I remained drunk, high, blacked out and numb at any and all costs.

In the public, I wore my makeup and smile displaying my happy clown exterior. Behind closed doors, the make-up got thicker and the tears of this clown fell.

I was orphaned and dying.

CHAPTER 9

Home Again?

Over the course of the next 6 ½ years, through my alcoholic sprees, acid trips and cocaine binges, one positive internal thing occurred during my personal insanity. This solitary ingredient, rooted in my motivation for personal healing, gave me a sort of hope and direction.

In my long, lonely nights, I began writing a song. Despite always finding a party and friends to share it with, I often found myself alone, either coming down off a high or continuing to party. I frequently became the only one left, attempting at all costs in continuing the party. Eventually, I was the only one that could appreciate my company. I didn't know much at the time; but somehow, I knew I had to write about my mother and father, commemorating their lives, family and home they provided to me and my brothers.

At that time, I believe my motivation was to honor my parents, not fully heal myself. No matter the motivation, I became addicted to the process of writing the song. In the song-writing process, sometimes I would write two words. Other nights I'd fill sheets of paper. Many papers and words, from the previous night's binge, hit the bottom of the wastebasket. Some became flammable. I crossed out, erased and changed words. My insane life appeared better while writing this song. Fixated on the process, I began caring less about the outcome of completing the song. Writing this song was my only saving grace or a semblance of a piece of peace in my chaotic life. Peace Through Music, the name of my current music business, was creeping in, but not even close to being solidified in my life.

After my father died, I vaguely remember only a few details of this sad afternoon. My three brothers, two of them having wives, and I gathered. The six of us stood in our parent's living room, holding hands, praying and saying our goodbyes to each other. I had no idea where I would end up that night. I knew I needed a drink, as my mourning escalated. Alcohol withdraw was settling upon me.

I don't remember what prayers or songs were recited. I remember feeling like this was it – the family was done and breaking up. Going our separate ways, unsure if even holidays would have us congregate. The initial contingency, pertaining to me, was that I was not permitted to stay in that house another night. I had burned my bridge. The four Brill sons would decide what to do with the house in the coming weeks. As we bid our goodbyes, I packed up some stuff and left. I cried profusely, as I walked down the street in one direction. Half way down the block I turned and walked the other way. I had no idea or destination today. It was the same ritualistic scenario for a long time.

Suddenly, a voiced yelled down the street. My head turning around was my fastest bodily function in months. It was my brother asking me to come back. Over and above my brothers' kind spirit, I believe the legacy of my parents was overwhelming. Although they knew it might be enabling and continuing the tradition of spoiling the youngest sibling, which they witnessed firsthand, my siblings decided to have me return to the house. They bequeathed to me yet another opportunity to rise to the occasion of opportunity, get my life together and grow up. In the finest of Mike Brill fashions, I took full advantage of this opportunity, by taking advantage of their love.

Music, drugs and alcohol consumed me the following months. The emerging façade, I was putting on for the public, quickly became a false reality to many. I was revealing my staggering reality of deterioration.

One night, at a performance, a lifelong friend who was taking a liking to the Jam Band/Grateful Dead atmosphere my band, Sizzlecat Sunshine, was providing, asked me if I wanted to get a place to live together. My friend had achieved so much in his life with a college degree and 4 years serving in the Navy. He was a proud firefighter. I had nothing, while selfishly waiting and wondering if I would financially profit from my dead parents' inheritance. I was ruthlessly malicious and selfish.

At the time, my friend was living in the neighborhood with his brother, above a bar which his brother owned. He said he was ready to get out and I needed a place to live. It was a perfect match. After searching and viewing some places, we settled on renting a home in Northeast Philadelphia. We rented it through my friend's work colleague. It was ideal for our living arrangement.

In the fall of 1997, move-in-day set the tone and tradition for this dwelling. Moving in became a three-day festival. My friend and new roommate probably second guessed his decision to move in with this lunatic. During the first day, we mounted a gifted plaque on the wall and christened our new home: The House of Bertha.

Bertha was a twin home with 3 bedrooms, living room, gas fireplace, dining room, kitchen, finished basement, two bathrooms and a backyard with a deck. The old deck was along the left side of the yard, where a pool once stood beside it many years prior. I think we are all thankful there was no pool. The catastrophic possibilities were endless.

The yard contained steel doors that lifted upwards to give direct access to the basement. I was in charge of the lawn care. Lawn care came easy to me with large quantities of Busch Beer and Grateful Dead music blaring from the radio. More often than not, the motivation of my green thumb efforts emerged from a cocaine surge.

We obtained a large tie-dye tapestry for our living room. It was a rainbow swirl hanging in the corner over our hand me down sectional couch donated from my parent's home. The artistic masterpiece orchestrated many fine visuals for the LSD parties. In the front picture window, overlooking the busy avenue, front lawn and pedestrians passing by, we hung a Grateful Dead banner. The clear and forward declaration of our home, draped in our front window, was complete with colorful dancing bears and a steal your face symbol born out of the rich artistic contributions and history of The Grateful Dead. We provided our neighbors and the public with no mystery of sight or sound of what was happening in our home.

Over the years, most likely during one of the many parties, people actually walked up our steps, knocked on our door and were granted entry into the insanity. I'm not sure they became lifelong "friends" but they left with a permanent memory of a moment in time that will resound fervently.

Those parties often lasted entire weekends. Imagine Animal House marrying Woodstock and the home the two established. That was the quintessence of The House of Bertha. One of our many, if not most famous party, had a live band in the backyard, one in the basement and jam sessions in the living room. Solo artists would supply tunes to the bedroom crowds. There were more musicians than listeners. We all took our turn doing both enthusiastically. That's one of the beautiful aspects of music. Music discriminates no one and includes each person as either a performer or appreciator. In music, one is the inspired or the inspiration. Both roles are crucial and dependent upon the other for music's ongoing existence and permanence.

A different person would show up at the party with different drugs throughout the party. I remember during the late '90's seeing and experiencing the influx of prescription pills, especially Percocet and Oxycotin. I partook and enjoyed them thoroughly when they came around. However, I don't remember searching for those drugs. And I searched for many. Every epidemic has a beginning and I was witnessing the opiate epidemic birth.

Each bedroom had its own mini party. The atmosphere of each bedroom was facilitated and sustained by the drug of choice of the occupants. Eventually, Nitrous Oxide tanks and LSD soon took the party into the nighttime and another dimension. I am not sure how many times the cops came, but somehow my roommate smoothed things over and kept the party going. We respected the neighbors to a certain degree. After all, when the night fell, we unplugged the instruments and came inside the house. We then filled the house with people, conversation, laughter and unplugged music for days. The house was a twin and to this day I have no idea how the neighbors next door survived or put up with our house party shenanigans. I don't even remember their names.

There were some quiet nights in the House of Bertha when TV became our entertainment. We were adults never getting enough of The Simpsons and King of the Hill. Somewhere there exists a journal with a list of every Simpson character. We also had a quote book, documenting some of the funniest things said in our house. At any moment, the insanity would stop at the drop of a dime, if what was said by someone was quote book worthy. Someone would document it immediately.

Throughout the years, we had gatherings of people turn to raging parties in the blink of an eye. The greatest times were when a chosen few of our closest friends gathered with nothing to do. We always found something to do and something to celebrate.

Most times it was before and after a live performance of our favorite Grateful Dead cover band *Splintered Sunlight*. Many of us loyal Deadheads would meet on Thursday nights at the House of Bertha to pile into as few cars as possible for safety purposes and caravan to Brownies 23 East in Ardmore, PA, where *Splintered Sunlight* performed weekly. Everyone knew everyone at these shows, even the band members. Still to this day, we call ourselves The Splintered Family. We've grown older together. We celebrated marriage and grieved the lives of the friends who have passed away. We watched the band change members. No matter what, most weeks had us catching the band live three or four nights in a row. Different songs and set lists each night; just like the Grateful Dead. If you closed your eyes, or opened them, it was the gift of the Dead's music rolled out on a red carpet and placed before us, as if we sat on a throne and deserved this musical genius. If the music was playing by this band we were there. The music never stopped; nor did we. Still today, I see *Splintered Sunlight* every chance I get.

The band even spearheaded ski trips. Buses of hippies and the band itself would reserve and invade a hotel near a ski slope. Rarely did any of us ski, due to the prioritization of massive partying superseding the placement of long, fiber glass footwear and risking our lives speeding down a snowcapped mountain. No, we had enough sense to risk our lives in the comfortable heated hotel, surrounded by our splintered family.

On the bus ride up to a ski trip, one of my best friends came into my life. He's been my closest friend and brother over the past 20 years. We have traveled the world and attended countless concerts together. He was and has always been there for me.

The band played two sets of music Friday; adding a third set on Saturday night. Between sets and after the actual shows, the party went from room to room. Each room contained a party and a free formed musical jam session. Guitar, singing and drum sounds filled the hallways of the hotel on a 24-hour continuum. The party began while getting on the bus near Philadelphia till the time we packed up and left the mountain hotel on Sunday, 2 days later. I don't know how we did it, but one year the legendary House of Bertha became an actual bus pick up destination for passengers of the renowned Splintered Ski Trip.

The intimate parties at the House of Bertha celebrating anything were the most memorable. A chosen few celebrated rain, sunshine, blizzards, birthdays, hurricanes and holidays which commanded our attention and respect. So, we partied accordingly. Those friends and memories, even while in long term sobriety, were paramount.

It's hard to remember, but over the years of our tenancy in the House of Bertha, my roommate and I welcomed at least 6 other tenants to live in our house. Rent became cheaper and the company was outstanding. Each added an element.

Those that crashed at our house after parties are too many to count. All were welcomed to a bedroom, couch, or floor under the ping pong table. When these guests awoke, more often than not, they found round 2, 3 or 4 of the party in full swing. Many people were still up and going from the night before. I was usually one of them that partied till I literally dropped. I could never get enough. Too much of anything wasn't enough. It was a head shaking tradition and we are all lucky to be alive.

Our house spawned relationships and love, with a few marriages still existing today. House of Bertha claimed friendships that will never end, despite many of us going our separate ways to fulfill our lives. We are alive and sharing in memories of our decadent party house, with many memories igniting shivers and head shakes, ultimately providing us with a bond that will never end. After my roommate got married, I unsuccessfully attempted to keep the house finances and tenants afloat.

As I look back on those times and often do reflect in sobriety, with the friends that shared those moments, we often weigh and share the insanity of those foggy permanent memories. Each of us has a different input or qualitative memory that makes the other person wonder how they missed that resounding moment. So many unforgettable moments to count, but with reflection come my demons and costly ongoing unhealthy decisions that led to my demise.

Even through the insanity, I was continuing to write my song.

Through the hard work I put into getting and remaining sober, after all of these years, I think back to the lack of dignity and respect I had for the legacy of my parents. My parents left me a decent inheritance. My selfish wish came true. Admirable and selfless parents in Northeast Philadelphia, who passed before their retirement and enjoyment of their earned Golden Years, working hard to keep a home, food on the table, Catholic school tuition, vacations, and keeping their kids active in every sport and activity possible, thought of their sons' future.

While living in the House of Bertha, I walked away from every career and educational opportunity I was provided. I never lost a job or got fired. My relentless ego provided me with the upper hand by losing jobs or not showing up before I got fired. In my selfishly created cognitions, everything was on my terms. I did everything to keep the upper hand in fine grandiose fashion.

I quickly put every cent of the thousands of dollars in inheritance up my nose or down my throat in party favors. These loving bequeathed funds, in a last loving gesture from parents through their hard-lifelong efforts, which were meant for me to get my shit together and grow up, fueled my Tears of a Clown persona. Everything was o.k. in my world, as I would have everyone believe.

When the money runs out, an alcoholic or addict becomes desperate. A different person emerges. At this point in my life, desperation was not a gift. Rather, it was the road to the end and the lowest I would go in my quarter century of living on this earth.

Presently, whenever I hear of severely publicized global or local events that happened during the time period of 1997-2003, I don't remember it happening. I don't know who won any of the championships of the major sport, even though I thoroughly enjoy sports. I don't recall the Olympics, elections, famous deaths or war. But I remember some of those hilarious quotes. At that time in my life, my world was dancing to music and partying inside and outside the walls of Bertha.

On the nights no one was around, I would still drink alcohol, drop acid, roll on ecstasy, pop pills and/or snort cocaine. I would write, erase and rewrite ingredients to my song. I was never disappointed in not finishing my song. In retrospect, I believe deep down, at that time, consciously or subconsciously at the core of my existence, I knew who I was. I was Mike Brill, the last son of Dot and Joe Brill and they taught me to be somebody. My dad's last words to me contained that message. His words and their purpose were creeping into my soul. Today I believe, we, as humans, were all meant to succeed.

God never made a nothing.

I needed to pay tribute to my parents and the only way I knew I was capable, was through a song. I wrote for the 4 plus years that I lived in the House of Bertha, but completed nothing. Consistent with the tradition of addictions, I failed at most things and completed nothing.

I still wrote.

Many years and ingredients of disorganized efforts went into this song creation. So many happy and sad times needed to happen for this song to be born. I was sober when it was completed.

Many years later, on a fateful day, June 30, 2003, after 6 ½ years of severe daily drinking and using drugs, I believe my parents and God provided me with my moment of clarity at 9:20am at the intersection of Torresdale and Cheltenham Aves. During a blackout, I found myself coming out of a 3-day binge. I was standing next to the playground, Moss A.A., where I grew up and played sports. To this day, I do not know how I got there or why I was provided with this moment of clarity at this special location of my childhood. The circle of life?

I looked in every direction, concluding I had no logical directional options that contained a productive destination. Instead, I called out and asked my God for help. I was out of questions, answers and opportunities. My decisions were devouring me. Bridges were burnt. I was exhausted. After sitting on the playground's single cement step at its entrance, crying and wishing I could hear my God's voice answering my plea, I got up and walked back down Torresdale Avenue.

I stopped into a diner for something to eat. Upon finishing my breakfast, I continued down the road, towards the home I grew up and terrorized. My brother was living there, himself in early sobriety.

Hope was finally a destination.

After a few steps and breaths, I disregarded the desperation, clarity and hope that crept in minutes before breakfast and I stepped into a corner bar and ordered a pint of beer. The neon signs in the bar window spelt defeat. Upon completion of my first pint and with a new pint already delivered by the bartender, I took both pints, one empty and one full, slid them to the end of the bar and with tears streaming down my face, I declared *"I'm done."*

Later that day, through the help of my brother, I went away for detoxification and treatment. My brother packed me a bag with his clothes and took me on SEPTA, Philadelphia public transportation, to my detox. My brother never left my side. I remember him saying to me words that resound in my life each day. He peacefully suggested: "Hey Mike, it might be time for you to open up your heart and mind to something new and let people in to help you." It stuck.

The next day in detox, July 1st, 2003, I breathed my first 24 hours of sobriety and have remained clean and sober ever since – over 16 years. Devine and spiritual parental intervention, next to Moss A.A. playground, where I grew up, kissed my first girl, played my sports and had my first beer; took this hopeless alcoholic out of a blackout into a world of possibilities and realities I could never have dreamed.

Weeks later, during in-patient treatment, as I lay in my single bed with my head up against a window that was jutting out in a turret of the Victorian home now housing and facilitating my rehabilitation from drugs and alcohol, I came to one of my first sane realizations. It was my first sober miracle. My mother and father had been dead over 6 years. During my first and (hopefully) last attempt at recovery and treatment in an Alcohol and Drug Rehabilitation Center, I was finally beginning to remember them and their truest essence.

In my second week of treatment, as I lay awake one night, the new client came into our bedroom from the bathroom. Five of us shared the bedroom comfortably. To this day, I don't know his name or even how long he lasted in treatment. He may have left the next morning or he might have been a figment of my imagination. He came into the room with his toiletries, blanking out the ceiling light with his massive frame. He was a biker and stood well over 6'5" containing 300 pounds of raw muscle. He was intimidating to say the least with his long straggly hair and tattoos covering every perceivable inch of his skin. I was bunking with Motorcycle Godzilla. But here we were with the same problems with a common destiny of stop using drugs and alcohol, while motivated to live life on life's terms.

As I pretended to be asleep, he did something that I see in my eyes and mind at this very moment. Even as I type this paragraph. I curiously squinted and soon had to double check my vision. My flickering eyes opened hesitantly. Was he kneeling at his bed? I couldn't tell at that moment as he kneeled at 5'8", a normal person's size. What was this massive biker dude doing? And then it happened. I vaguely heard murmurs of praise and prayer coming from his mouth. My eyes finally adjusted to the bedroom's darkness and the moon became my provincial source of light. His hands were folded tightly like a second-grade Catholic school boy making his first communion. He prayed, bowed and cried. Moreover, this massive and outlandish biker brought me to my Higher Powers.

I laid awake most of the night wondering what I had just seen. The next morning, I woke early and remained in bed with a spiritual hangover. In my 33 years of life, I don't ever recall having one of its kind. My holy, prayerful biker friend was already off starting the day, a freshly made bed in his rear-view mirror. He may have left treatment because I don't remember having the chance to thank him. Unbeknownst to him, he became my inspiration providing me with the courage to permit myself to begin my journey of prayer, spirituality and a connection to a Higher Power that I sustain daily.

On that steamy hot July morning, before getting out of bed and starting my day, I said "good morning Mom and Dad." I began to cry.

This daily morning salutation to my Mother and Father is the permanent and consistent cornerstone to my spirituality. Finally, I'm allowing my parents to help me. The trauma of losing them 6 ½ years prior, within 8 months of each other, had been saturated with booze and drugs. It was time to make them and their passing an asset in my life, not a liability. I focused on their lives, not their deaths. My newly constructed trauma narrative stars my Mother and Father and their abundant blessings bestowed upon me.

My parent's legacy is a staple of my sober life, and I had to thank them. My song needed to be finished. Responsible sober people finish what they start. Rationalization and justifications took an about face, productive turn in my life. After solidifying sobriety through ongoing hard and emotional work, I began hearing and living by the statement: "You have to give it away to keep it." This is the only command of sobriety in most pathways of holistic recovery programs. Don't tell me you're grateful, rather, show me you are grateful by helping others.

Gratitude is an action word and its' outcome is earned through engagement and achievement of its motion reality. The action of recovery gratitude is helping another human being. Give away sobriety freely to others, so that I might maintain my own. This is a beautiful reality of selfless and selfish action working in coordination. When gratitude is performed, helping others creates a Utopia, a perfect world. I needed to apply this philosophy to my song.

I don't know the date, place or time I put down the pen, but the song was complete. The last stroke of my pen was the question mark in the title of my song: *Home Again?* The question mark signifies my commitment to live my life as long as possible; help as many people; and make a lasting impression on this world up to the time when I depart and reunite with my parents in our paradise.

I wanted to die every day and now I wanted to live and contribute.

My tribute to my parents, family and home on Cottage Street was finally a song born out of universal perceptions of death and life, addictions and recovery. I married the positive to the negative and let it fester, while guiding my creation. Death and life are experienced by everyone. I wanted to tap that universality and through my song provide others the opportunity to reflect on their own lives, grief and healing. I was giving away my song, so that I may fully experience its gift of healing to me. I have performed this song for many years and it still blows me away to hear people request it by name: *Home Again?*

Through the voice of my father and the tenderness of my mother
I've become that man I am today
I've become the proud lad that I am today
My thanks to them are endless and my gratitude is sincere
My loving will be forever, still wishing
They were here

Wondering wishing never knowing
Where that golden road will lead us onto

Just remembering and cherishing the times
We've been through

Those were the times we took so many pictures
And the times we sang so many songs
They were the times we hurt
And the others we cried
That made our house a home

Well I know that sometime we'll all be together
Though I wish it was here and right now
It's a selfish thought from a hurting son
And I know me brothers feel the same no doubt

Wondering wishing never knowing
Where that golden road will lead us onto
Just remembering and cherishing the times
We've been through

Just one more Christmas together
Another St. Patrick's Day
One more birthday celebration
Just another time we can all be together
Another second together
In our home on
Cottage Street

Through the voice of my father and the tenderness of my mother
I've become that man I am today
I've become the proud lad I am today

Copywrite: Mike Brill, 2005
(Through explorer browser you can hear a live version of this song: www. mikebrill.com/music)

CHAPTER 10

The College Kid

Abstinence, not picking up and consuming the first drink or drug, is not sobriety. From abstinence all things are possible. It is the core foundation and beginning to something greater. Science has conditioned animals to stop using drugs. I'm not a monkey or lab rat. I am human and as an addict and alcoholic, stopping was not enough. Action in change was vital to becoming a productive citizen and the person I always wanted to be.

If acceptance brings forth the dire need for abstinence, it should than initiate the memory of an unmanageable life, that contains unsuccessful efforts in controlling that addiction and managing one's life. The solution does not exist in an addict. The addiction lifestyle and progression are the living, real, and re-confirmed proof of this staggering fact. Eventually, it blossoms from the individual through changing and adopting new thoughts and behaviors. I remember a man telling me that I don't get any more sober, after 35 days of sobriety. He then proceeded to tell me that he would help me learn how to live. Learning how to live sober and productively, with meaning and purpose, is sobriety. I was ready to get busy living.

A lifelong friend nicknamed me The College Kid. It became an ongoing funny and real reminder of my longevity and lack of success in Higher Education. I lived like a college kid most of my adult life. Peter Pan had nothing on me. The party always had to go on and educational success did not fit into that agenda. While not going to college the entire time, it took me 19 years and finally at age 37, I obtained my Bachelor's

Degree. My friend still calls me The College Kid. It just stuck and since he's my lifelong buddy, I smile each time I hear it.

My last class to obtain my Bachelor's Degree at LaSalle University was Anthropology. After 5 unsuccessful attempts at completing my higher education, I had come to my final hurdle. Three credits and 16 weeks of classes declared my finish line. I was still a kid wrapped in fear of success and failure. There I was 4 years sober and still just existing on the equator, being o.k. while afraid of success.

On the first day of class, a young man in kakis, flip flops and surfer, dirty blonde hair walked into the classroom. He placed an old leather brief case on the table, wrote his name on the board and proceeded to introduce himself as our professor. I thought he was a student. Although in disbelief that this dude was teaching me, immediately I somehow knew everything was going to be alright.

I adore people, culture and traditions. I have a lasting thirst for its knowledge, especially experientially. I've come to believe cultures' greatest gift and asset is the confirmation of one's own identity. Through learning about other cultures, we become secure and proud in our own. The teacher reviewed the 3-part syllabus, identifying three ethnographies that the class would be exploring. Oh great, this means three more textbooks to purchase. Those were my three greatest textbooks. I still have them today.

The first ethnography was The Gebusi Tribe of Papua New Guinea. The Gebusi Tribe was as primitive, forest dwelling tribe as you could find in modern times. Luckily, a scientist and his wife were permitted to live amongst them to provide their readers and cultural fanatics a primary source of their daily culture and traditions. The textbook is more like a story than a classroom resource.

The second ethnography was about the people and culture in the Land of the Gods: The Balinese in Bali, Indonesia. Bali is part of an archipelago. Indonesia is a country situated between the Indian and Pacific oceans. It is the world's largest island country, with more than thirteen thousand islands. Scientists claim they are still discovering and counting Indonesian islands. Indonesia is the world's 14th largest country in terms of land mass and the 7th largest in terms of combined sea and land area. While the prominent religion of Indonesia is Islam, Hinduism in Indonesia, is practiced by 1.7% of the total population. The majority of Bali's population, 83.5%, practice Hinduism.

This tiny tear drop of an island, truly is the land of the Gods. Each person in Bali believes they have a connection to royalty born from the migrating royalty from India. This tropical paradise, combined with the outward practices of faith and dedication to the Gods, manifests this third world island as a catalyst towards inner strength and transformation of mind, body and soul. This enlightenment is available for any human being to experience, if they are willing. The text, professor and eventually the Balinese people changed my life forever, because I willingly invited them into my world.

The third cultural lesson, and the teacher's bread and butter, due to it being the topic of his doctoral thesis, was the Rastafarian culture and philosophy. I came back to this textbook many years later for further enlightenment. I remember during this last portion of the class, I had one foot out the door. In my mind, I slacked and was already graduated. Maybe subconsciously, I was so riveted and changed by the first two ethnographies, that I was lacking the responsible attention of a 19th year college student.

The professor had his own first-hand experiences complete with a slide show of his time spent in Trinidad and Tobago living amongst the Rastafarians. He took part in building and implementing a social and educational program. Rastafarian isn't all cannabis and music. Those are merely vessels of enlightenment provided by Jah. Like the Gebusi Tribe and Balinese, the collective and individual stoic dedication and ongoing reverence to faith, community and family is a lesson needed to be embraced, respected and shared by all.

There is a living insecurity and battle within myself concerning my lack of commitment. Is it a personality trait or character flaw? Perhaps, I have a lack of commitment combined with an intense interest in other cultures, religions and traditions. My living mantra has become the reality and asset that *I do not say no to any bit of knowledge or experience, mine or others, that can help me not harm myself or others with my thoughts, words or actions; one day at a time.* And if I do harm, in my imperfection as a human, every religion or culture that I've come to embrace, believes in the grace of forgiveness towards self and others. I must be humble and willing to pursue such an awesome act of human and Godly kindness.

I've heard the saying that people save the best for last. This final class of my Bachelor's Degree was just that: The Best! As I sat in that final class, taking my final exam, with each question that I answered tears welled up. I was the oldest person in the class, feeling like a 7-year-old. Was this really happening? Was I to become a college graduate after 19 years of attempts and failures? I received an A for the class, but I never received my final exam back and I was always curious if I got the last question correct. Please don't ask me the question or the answer.

All I remember is at that very moment in time, my only concern was for no other students to be disturbed by my full-on crying, while holding back the hyperventilation. No matter what, the Gebusi Tribe, Balinese and Rastafarian people and subject matter, of my last 16 weeks, were now in the books; but never to be forgotten. The lessons and inspiration have become a huge asset in the construction of my spirituality.

I walked to the front of the classroom, where my professor sat at the desk respectfully monitoring the test process. Admirably, he was absorbing new knowledge from a book he was reading. My tears were tumbling, snot was flowing freely, and the guarded hyperventilation gave way to infantile farm animal noises. The professor noticed. Most likely, I was a blur to him; as I was in dire need of freedom and escape embarrassment. He followed me out the door and called for me in my race to the bathroom or building exit. I couldn't see through the tears. The professor's approachability and real mannerisms, combined with true professionalism, led him to this interaction with a crying student. This was not in his job description.

I can only imagine his thirst for teaching and developing minds were already engrained on his young soul and career. "Hey Mike, what's up? Are you alright?" I managed words and a few incomplete sentences. But quickly, the 16 weeks of hanging on his every word, put me at ease and quickly I engaged him with my story.

I told him about the 19 years of vain educational attempts, my parents' deaths, my progression of addiction leading to homelessness and hopelessness. It was the most concise reflection of my insane, traumatic life that I ever verbalized to another human being. His attention was enough. However, adding words of congratulations, while endlessly appreciated, were too minimal for him. He presented me a statistical fact with which I walked into my Master's Program and carry with me each day. On that May evening in 2007, he informed me I was now a part of 1% of the world's population. Only one percent of the world's population had obtained a Bachelor's Degree. Now, my tears were truly tears of pride. I was afforded another piece of the puzzle towards my identity, built upon positive self-regard.

Eleven years later, 2018, while writing this book, as I was talking on the phone with my cousin about her son's mission trip for Spring Break, the cosmos provided me yet another gift of connectivity. So many beautiful opportunities to connect the dots. As she described her son's trip with great pride and detail, where her son would travel to a Caribbean Island to volunteer at a community building. She further mentioned the Island: Trinidad and Tobego and the cool professor that was spearheading this voyage of a lifetime. Furthermore, she shared about her son's bond with this real and approachable professor. This, ironically, was in her son's last semester of college.

We mutually googled the university staff. Quickly, it was confirmed, exactly what I was thinking. Serendipitously, my last inspirational undergraduate professor, who taught me in my last class of Anthropology, 11 years prior, when I learned about people and culture in a way never experienced, was now my little cousin's professor. I didn't know I could become more excited for my cousin's Spring Break. I never forgot that professor. I can't imagine nor could I wish for a better way of being reminded of this professor's gifts.

Once a teacher always a teacher; even on Spring Breaks or in hallways outside the classroom in the commencement of final exams. He taught and inspired me to embrace people, firsthand.

Oh, the places you'll go.

CHAPTER 11

Right Of Passage

As I finished my Bachelor's Degree, the challenges, as they often do, even in success, clouded those previously experienced vital life lessons. My dots were not being connected in order to see the big picture. As I was working full time at The Hospital of the University of Pennsylvania, I applied for every appropriate job, within and outside the organization. Armed with a Bachelor's Degree, during that time, I received only one phone interview. The statistical fact of being 1% of the world's population was blurred by the reality of the depreciating value of a Bachelor's Degree in America. That real dot pushed me forward, in another direction.

I began applying for Master's Degree Programs. The tuition benefit at my work was the Rolls Royce of benefits and who am to argue with the first-class blessings bestowed upon me through gainful employment. My defeatist outlook of self and the world was combated by embracing a golden opportunity. I took it and followed through.

I applied to two graduate programs and was accepted to both. With the letters in each hand, I sat on my couch wondering if the institutions knew I was a bum in the park, sleeping under leaves, back porches and benches throughout the city of Philadelphia. Everything in my life revolved around remaining drunk and high. After all I thought, isn't that what college kids do?

Positive self-esteem is mostly challenged in finding worthiness of success. I still didn't feel worthy. The mind has a compass of its own and the personal challenge is confirming or denying its directional patterns based on self-worth. I was approaching 4 years of sobriety and achieved so much in my life. Yet, here I am with achievements in hand, still doubting my worthiness of acceptance and triumph. I quickly became the captain of my brain; and navigated this anchor of self-doubt.

There were more lessons involved, courtesy of my friend, Tom. I showed him my acceptance letters. I displayed them with great pride. He endlessly congratulated me and asked me when I needed to make my decision of choosing a school and program. I told him that I had already made up my mind. Tom quickly negated that decision-making-model with an invaluable lesson. He redirected me to his original question, pertaining to the time frame of my decision.

He lassoed me and brought me back to our original conversation and I responded that I have approximately two months to make my decision. He told me to go home tonight, fold up the two acceptance letters and put them in the back of my sock drawer.

He proceeded to advise. Tom said, I want you to live each day moving forward, for the next two months, knowing and cherishing that you have the freedom to choose today; a choice. He reminded me of the times I had no choice or freedoms. The times, I was a slave to substances and the plan of that substance was to rip away every fiber of my being and existence. I now had a situation of deliberation; where my choices were two blessings. Both were enriched with a guaranteed win-win process and outcome. My freedom was reconfirmed on a daily basis. Freedom's reality is truly a vital ingredient to building rapport with oneself.

After swimming in freedom and then choosing to attend Holy Family University, I entered the Counseling Psychology Program with a concentration in Student Affairs. Immediately, I began to portray a meteorologist, in my ridiculous and vain attempts in giving a ten-day forecast; when rarely knowing what's going to happen tomorrow. One day (one thought, one lesson and one breath) at a time became vital. It's amazing how this little phrase and slogan can eliminate the internal mysterious battles of indecision and insecurity.

As I approached the summer of 2007, while still working full time, without the pressures of keeping up with the demands of part time schooling, my mind began to wander. One day at a time does not apply when dreaming, setting goals or paying bills. Our goals connect the innocence of a child to our adult responsibilities. My innocence, at all costs, had been doused by years of adult human avoidance. I was consumed, wondering if I would ever get a weekend at the beach, after I started my Master's program. I thought about traveling and making plans for a huge, memorable journey. As the dreams and planning got clouded with insecurity and doubt, my self-esteem lowered. I fought back by remembering how far I've come and what I've achieved. But a big trip by myself? Where would I go?

I've never gone far alone and only once have I traveled west of the Mississippi. That was with my best friend, Padraig, visiting my friend, Rusty, in California in 2005. I was 2 years sober. Rusty had been living out there for some years now and was established as an Orange County citizen of music. He set me up with a bed, music gigs, and some of them revolved around joining in with his band, The West Coast Strays. After a hero's welcome and royal hospitality by his family and friends, we proceeded to golf by day and played music each night.

Finally, after 14 years of playing music, I'd arrived as sober "rock star," if only in my own mind and for only a week. It was enough to prove that I was capable and worthy, au natural, of sober fun and experiences in any capacity, especially music.

The highlight of the West Coast tour/trip was an outdoor benefit concert on The Pacific Coast Highway in Orange County. Hurricane Katrina had just occurred and the entire nation was coming to New Orleans' aid. You couldn't turn around and not bump into a musician, famous ones even. At times, there were 15 musicians on stage. During jam sessions, my friend, Rusty, would call me up to the stage, mid-song, give me his guitar, whisper the chords in my ear and include me in the jam session.

One such jam, later in the afternoon, involved the classic long-lasting jam, *In A Gadda Da Vidda*, by Iron Butterfly. The song is so long I believe every musician in the place got a chance to perform during this rendition. My friend blessed me with that opportunity. I jumped up on stage without hesitation. Rusty whispered the chords to me and added the ingredients of a musical memory I will not ever forget. As I was attempting to keep up with the song, he told me to look over my right shoulder. I was jamming next to Lee Dorman, the original bassist for Iron Butterfly. Banging the drums, jamming behind was the touring drummer for Eddie Money. Off to my left was the keyboardist of The Animals. It was a surreal moment that benefited a great cause. I was O.K. at that moment, though its memory, continues to radiate as one of my fondest musical memories.

Eventually, my pre-masters traveling research led me to a cruise or hiking in Alaska. A solo American voyage, to a land in our country that I've only heard about, as the 48th state. Or was it 49th or 50th? Alaska's physical detachment from continental America, made it an adventure, an uncomfortable one at that. Getting uncomfortable to get comfortable is a pathway to personal conquest and acceptance. As all of the trips were researched, on various websites, I filled out many forms, only to disembark on the confirmations. I could not brave hitting enter and make up my mind and feel worthy. I was scared.

It was during these hesitations that my reflection on educational achievement, demands of a master's program and the mantra of getting uncomfortable to get comfortable, guided me to my unforgettable class and teacher of Anthropology. The Caribbean Islands were too close and the Gebusi Tribe of Papua New Guinea too mysterious and remote.

However, the Balinese appealed to me. I've always had a fond admiration for the longevity and natural aspects of Eastern Philosophies. This interest was possibly born out of the Western philosophical ignorance towards this holistic pathway of life. Pathways to solutions of wellness are everywhere and should be accessible to everyone. Finances should not exclude opportunity or promotion of wellness. I am and continue to be fascinated by Eastern philosophies and practices in natural human and earth-born ingredients and processes. Time and duration have proven the reliability of Eastern philosophies of living and healing as a productive and natural existence.

As I embarked on researching The Land of the Gods, Bali Indonesia, I realized I would not be in Kansas (or in my case Philadelphia) anymore. The travel itself would be nerve-wracking and brutal. The three planes, almost two-day journey with crossing time zones, seemed to hover over as a deterrent to this trip. After researching further, I came up with the brilliant idea to take an intercontinental flight direct to Los Angeles. I would than board my one layover flight to Tapai, Taiwan and then onto Bali, Indonesia. I felt more secure going the Western route.

At the time, I was still working at Penn Medicine. On the day of my trip, I worked a half day. Coworkers offered to drop me off at the Philadelphia airport. In the months prior to the trip, I could feel the rising anxiety of coworkers, friends and family towards my solo trip East. As if my own anxiety wasn't enough, I had to relieve others of theirs'. The convincing reinforced my decision.

On departure day, anxiety riddled me like a Gatling gun. I quickly referred to this trip as my rite of passage, a necessary tool to emerge from its experience as man, an autonomous being with authentic experiences few others gravitate towards or accomplish. I had achieved so much and was ready for more experiences and education that would make me more whole.

I entered work that day with my bags packed and a nasty head cold brewing. My excuses, to use my trip insurance to cancel the trip, were becoming too tangible. The rewards of partaking in the trip triumphed over the emerging excuses. A fever began and I perceived the next two days and 26 hours of plane encapsulated travel as my worst pending nightmare scenario.

On the car ride to the Philadelphia Airport, my coworkers literally asked me outright if I still wanted to go. Armed with vitamin C, cold medicine and large quantities of American currency to buy fruit and whatever else would alleviate this ripping cold, I responded to my coworkers, without hesitation, that this was now something I had to do and nothing could stop me.

Reporting to the airport three hours before travel, I experienced a seamless pathway to my gate. I had plenty of time to be nervous and heal. My books, diary and snacks kept me busy in the Southwest Airlines terminal gate. However, my anxiety drove me to wander throughout the terminal.

I went from store to store looking for the things I didn't forget. I ate oranges and apples like they were falling off the trees onto my lap. I lapped the terminal a dozen times. As the time approached for boarding, I was feeling excited and proud of myself.

As I wandered back to my gate, from my last walkabout, 50 yards ahead of me there was an adult bending down, giving directions or scolding a young girl of about 5 years of age. There appeared to be an urgency to the elder's dialogue directed towards the girl. As I approached, our eyes attached like a sci-fi ray beam. As the young girl's eyes and the boarding time pulled me closer, I noticed she had Down Syndrome. I slowed my pace while fueled by my curiosity of the conversation. Soon, the words were stifled and unimportant. Energy had been established.

I felt as if the little girl was talking to me without saying a word. It was quickly apparent that her caregiver/parent's words were not even penetrating her, whatsoever. My pace slowed, but never stopped, and nothing else mattered at that moment in time. I forgot I was in an airport, heading to Asia.

As I approached this beautiful young person, my anxiety and head cold ceased to exist. Her eyes were aligned with my eyes; as her head turned towards me in seamless synchronicity, like the gears inside a tower clock. It was perfect 4/4 timing – her eyes and my eyes, and her head with my feet. Harmony, with no lyrics. As I was passing her, the girl's head twisted with every step I took, like we knew each other our entire lives. Now, as I passed her slowly, my head was twisting back to her, almost 180 degrees. If there was a cliff in front of me, I would have walked off the edge. Each step I took increased the magnetism created between our eyes. I paused in simultaneous confusion and enlightenment. I forgot about my gate, plane and rite of passage for what seemed like days.

My pause ignited her gift to me - a simple smile that spoke volumes. With this little girl's nonverbal communication of a smile, somehow this young stranger told me I was going to be alright and that this rite of passage, trip of a lifetime, is what's meant to happen in my life at that very moment. A feeling of confidence, security and permission I have rarely felt swept over me. I became the recipient of the innocence of a child, permitting me to live my life in experiencing the goodness of the world that lay out before me. I turned and cried my way to the gate. I felt relieved and comfortable in every step after that moment. Anxiety disappeared, knowing I would be safe on my journey.

My 6-hour flight to Los Angeles International Airport (LAX) was seamless and comfortable. I began my journal with the smile from my new friend. As the plane descended, approaching the west coast landing, I felt my heart racing and head cold bubbling, dreading the 5 ½ hour layover in the international wing of LAX airport. I settled in for a nap after two oranges, vitamin C and whatever cold medicines I could consume.

As boarding started for my 14 ½ hour China Airlines flight to Tapai, Taiwan, the second leg of my trip, I added up that I've been a citizen of airports and air travel for 14.5 hours already.

As I sat on the ground Indian style, an Asian family of 16 caught my eye. From the estimated age parameters, I was guessing there were four generations present. As the seats for boarding were being called by airline officials, movement began within the family that was filled with resounding mutual care and concern. The eldest, possibly approaching a hundred years of age, was the focus of the family's attention. From the family looking and pointing, I realized the elder had to go to the bathroom. There was not a glint of concern for the seats being called or the urgency of boarding an international flight back home or visiting family in their homeland. The strategy and dedication towards this elder family member's needs were all that mattered.

The youngest family member, 4 or 5 years of age, held the great-great grandmother's hand, while four other family members walked beside the aging woman. The elder was not going alone, externally displaying and encapsulating the love and dedication of a collective society's primary mission. Four generations walked this elderly woman to the bathroom facilities, at her pace, with love and disregard for whatever was to happen with their flight and travels.

I am a proud Irish American with a gift of amazing parents who provided cultural and family pride. But, as an individual and society, we have so much to learn within the realms of collective prioritization and family values. This airport classroom and its single student, me, was provided a lesson, from this family, that I will never forget. Moreover, this lesson prepared me for Eastern Philosophy lessons to come. At that moment, I forgot I was still in The United States of America.

After 14.5 brutal hours of flying to Tapai, Taiwan, I emerged from the plane exhausted. I entered the Taiwan Taoyuan International Airport and dropped into a lounge chair for my 4-hour layover. I feel asleep immediately. I awoke just a half hour later and looked around. The airport floors glistened in the sunlight. Not realizing where I dropped to sleep, I was shocked that I was in a recliner, surrounded by earthly creations within an Asian garden setting. I looked up to just confirm there was a roof above my head. It was a sunroof providing the gift of sunlight to my present garden airport residence.

I strolled to the toilets, as they call them in Asia, and experienced the cleanest bathroom I ever witnessed. I could have sat down and had a picnic lunch in this pristine bathroom. I wished I could have stayed and witnessed Taiwan, but it will have to stay on my list of places to go. Bali was waiting just 5 ½ more hours away. Boarding, for my third flight, in my second day of travel, had begun.

While delirious on the last flight, I heard the announcement of approaching landing. I woke up in an instant, preparing for my landing and truly the start of my vacation. Out the window, I searched for land. There was none, yet the plane was dropping elevation. As the plane got closer to the waters of the Indian Ocean, my heart raced. I thought we were making a water landing. Finally, a tiny island surrounded by crystal blue waters appeared. The airport runway in Bali's capital, Depensar, started at the edge of the island.

As I emerged from the plane, I entered the airport. It was a hut with a hay roof. The open air spaced airport was like nothing I had ever seen. I swam through the foreign language echoing around me and went through Customs, with my 30-day visa. It was surreal.

In preparation of my trip, I researched temple tours, golf courses, holistic healing seminars, hotels, flights, money exchange, culture and religions. During the era of Myspace, I chatted with Balinese men and women in the hopes of obtaining firsthand advice of the country's traditions and people. I met one of those persons in Bali for lunch and I am still friends with her, now on Facebook.

As others' concern rose and was verbalized, safety became a frequent Google search. No amount of research could have prepared me for the experiences that were soon to become a reality. A third world's environment and economy, that lies in the arms of tourism, is plentiful with business' attempts at experiential hospitality and ultimately financial gain. Where there is financial gain, there is self-willed greed. I researched and proceeded cautiously. I focused on booking trips to various temples that included authentic opportunities to engulf myself into the Balinese Hindu traditions.

Again, the rich and proud folk tradition is that each Balinese person believes they stem from Indian royalty. They treated me equally. Despite

Dutch and English conquests and revolutions, Bali appears to be an independent paradise; unique to its own religion and culture. Their outward display of shrines and dedication to the Gods lives on every door step of businesses and homes. They even present offerings on the dashboards of motor vehicles. Harmony and balance are everywhere. My personal quest for serendipity, harmony and balance began well before landing in Bali.

As family and friends communicated their concerns for me, while they slipped in contrasting thoughts of excitement, I spoke with my brother in great length about my knowledge and lessons learned in my last undergrad class at LaSalle University. He proceeded to tell me of his soccer league that was formed by many foreign players who have settled in the Lehigh Valley, PA. They have embraced the opportunity to continue their tradition and culture of playing their sport, football (Soccer in America). He verbalized an assumption that possibly a few of the players were from Indonesia. He referred to one player, named *Made*. My eyes lit up as he pronounced the name with American consistency; just how its sounds in English (MAID). However; "*Made*" (pronounced Mah-day in Balinese) is the name given to the second child born in a Balinese household.

In general, Balinese families name their children according to birth order. The names are the same for both males and females. The firstborn child is named *Wayan*; the second is named *Made*; the third child goes by *Nyoman*; and the fourth is named Ketut. The fifth child would return to the beginning, giving the first and fifth child the same name. *Made*, now living in the Lehigh Valley is the second born in his Balinese household. Throughout my trip, I was Ketut Mike, the fourth born in my family.

After providing my brother a lesson in Balinese family name culture, he promised efforts towards connecting me with *Made*. As luck would have it, *Made* responded to my email, while he was traveling the world. After a few correspondences and letting Made know the confirmed dates of my trip, serendipity breathed another chapter to my trip. At the end of *Made's* trip, he was returning to Bali to visit family. As luck would have it, he would be there for my first three days of the trip. We constructed plans to meet and exchanged phone numbers.

On the third day of my trip in Bali, I had a tour which consisted of whitewater rafting through the rainforest of Bali. The dry season gave way to a simpler chore of navigating the less than rough waters. I was teamed up with couples from Japan and Russia. I was solo, and yet again, I was to be introduced to another person named *Made*, our boat and tour guide. Unfortunately, I was floored with jet lag that morning. Throughout the day, it only got worse. Rough waters, literally and figuratively, were in my dreaded future. I was scheduled to meet my brother's soccer mate, *Made*, later that day.

Upon arrival back to my hotel, I phoned *Made* to let him know of my exhausted condition and the need for a nap. He understood and he agreed to meet me at my hotel at 4:30pm. Concluding my nap, I was a new man upon his arrival. I was nervous to meet and spend time with a native Balinese. Again, the stars aligned. Unbeknownst to me, *Made's* home was in the village of Sanur, 4 minutes from my hotel. An entire island and thousands of hotel options to book my accommodations, before knowing of *Made*, and I was literally in his neighborhood.

His warmth and hospitality were overwhelming – just a downright cool dude. Hospitably, he immediately asked me what I wanted to do and I did not hesitate to respond in the hopes of first hand witnessing the fruition and authentication of my textbook and classroom learning.

First, I wanted to see his home. His home was beautiful and complete with bed pillows signifying his family members sleeping with their heads facing the mountains representing a dedication to the Gods. Feet faced the waters; where the lower powers or demons exist. Up represents good, down is bad. He allowed me to play authentic Balinese instruments: drums, xylophones etc. We sat and talked by his majestic garden surrounded by offerings to the Gods. The water from his infinity pool was constantly flowing over the edges, giving off a resounding stream of continuous peacefulness of tranquility and harmony.

As words decreased and time went forward into the early night, welcomingly he asked me what else I would like to do. Without hesitation, I asked if it was the Full Moon. He was taken back by my thirst for furthering my knowledge and interest in his culture. However, inquisitively he wondered out loud what was my interest in the Full Moon. The Full Moon or *Purnama* is a sacred Hindu Balinese celebration that involves all Hindu Temples celebrating and praising the Gods and Mother Earth. I had no idea of the ingredients, but I told *Made* that I wanted to partake. Again, he wrapped his generous arms around this request and stated we have to get ready and then you can join me and my family for the celebration.

My new friend, *Made*, supplied me with authentic Balinese formal clothes, complete with a formal silk sarong wrapped around my informal sarong. During formal ceremonies, men wear both types of sarongs. He supplied me with Hindu head wear and a Batik white Balinese shirt. If it wasn't for my sneakers and the map of Ireland on my face, I might have passed for a Balinese Hindu. Either way, internally, I was Hindu.

After a few pictures, the family and I piled into a car and the conversation was refreshing; even while not knowing a single word they were saying. Maybe they were critiquing my outfit or wondering why this American is always smiling. My smile was perpetual. Either way, their entire *banjar*, a collective term for a community of people in Bali, embraced me for the next 15 hours of my life; celebrating, praying, eating and dancing; paying homage to the Gods of the Full Moon. Without illicit substances in my system, I have never been awake and so happy in my entire life.

Brill dressed and ready for the Hindu Festival - Purnama Sashsadha

The *Purnama* ritual took place in three connecting, open air temples. Through the entrance, a *gamelan*, a Balinese orchestra, resounded traditional songs. There were about 30 pieces of instruments. Each musician sat on the floor and played beautifully. The volume of unique musical sounds filled my heart and the volume blew my hair back. Yet, not one instrument was plugged into electronics.

The first section of the temple contained a canteen of sorts; where an abundance of fruit, rice and non-alcoholic drinks were supplied by the community. We passed through the dinning/social area and walked across a rice paddy field leading us into the second section of the temple. Incense and natural aroma of flowers and spices filled the air. Not a word was spoken; as I sat down on the ground, cross legged, to begin my praying. *Made* sat next to me, and noticed the tears filling my eyes. I was overflowing with a cultural and religious privilege I'd never experienced. There was no cadence or collective repetition in their praising of the Gods. It was an individual journey coupled with the simple warmth and reality found in the community of others. I was stiff with mystery of whether I was doing "it" right.

As a priest came around to my new *banjar, Made's* family, he instructed me to reach in the bowl and place sticky rice on my forehead's third eye position and one clump on each side of my temples. The holy rice really stuck during the entire celebration. The next person had a bowl with incense scented water. In the bowl laid fresh flowers. I was instructed to take the water-soaked flower with my fingers and drip it onto my head and shoulders - a baptism of sorts.

In the recognized Catholic tradition, *Made* asked me to follow his routine of holding his hands together in prayer at mouth level. I proceeded, shaking with a warm holistic feeling of healing. He took his hands and raised them above his head, towards the sky. After a pause he brought them back to his mouth level. Another pause gave way to an outward movement of the hands, fingertips pointing forward, away from the chest.

After a dozen or so reps of me playing follow the leader, *Made* explained to me that this prayer sequence was first praying for yourself (hands at mouth), who must praise and give thanks to God(s) (upward motion). Hands brought down to the mouth represented the gifts and dedication of the Gods to self. The outward motion signifies my dedication, energy and connection to the world. Self, God, Self, World, back to Self. I pray for self, through invested energy towards a Higher Power. That Higher Power is energy. My faith is that my Higher Power will give back to me, so that

I might induce better decisions towards making the world a better place. In Karmic tradition, what I supply to the world, will be returned to me.

Brill at Festival preparing for prayer with his new Banjar

I thought of my late father's mantra during those moments of reverence and prayer. My father believed and proclaimed: *I am third – God, Family than Self.* I reminisced on their lifelong dedication to the Catholic Church and their beloved parish of St. Bartholomew's in Northeast Philadelphia. My mother lived in the same parish throughout her entire life, graduating from St. Bart's and Little Flower High School. They were amazing people that raised a wonderful family; rich with faith, friendships, memories and honor. St Bartholomew School has closed and is now a nursing home with no affiliation to the church. The remaining church structure contains many memorials with the names and spirit of my mom and dad. They loved that church and their action in faith and community reinforced that love and dedication.

I couldn't help wonder if my parents would mind that I was sitting and praying in a Hindu Temple, 10,000 miles away from home. I assumed if it was helping me stay sober, they'd agree with anything that helped me.

My spirituality now contained another ingredient. I would never be the same again from this authentic Hindu celebration. From the thought of my parents, their faith, my sobriety and so many other ingredients; I have developed a mantra that has helped me stay sober and productive in my life. I often tangle with this thought presuming I am noncommittal in my religious affiliation.

However, again my mantra states; *I do not say no to anything that is going to help me avoid harming myself or others with my thoughts, words or actions, one day at a time.* Let me reiterate: I take from all religions, historians, parents, neighbors, friends, coaches and especially the experiential education I thrust myself into every chance that I get. These sources of energy provide me the ingredients of making better decisions. I have traveled the world and I am not done. I have read books and I'm not done. I've played and written music and I'm not done. I'm never done and this is the reality I want to create for my own spiritual development. A permanent open heart and mind creates opportunity.

The Full Moon Ceremony rarely stood still, even in prayer. I was permitted a camera in the temples. I must have taken 500 pictures. I witnessed families creating and presenting beautiful shrines and offerings to the Gods. Traditional Balinese music filled the air; as formal and informal dances and movements swept by me. It was over 95 degrees and their simple dedicated dancing gave me arctic chills. The culture's breath was simultaneous with each heartbeat. The vibrant colors resembled a parking lot at a Grateful Dead concert – rainbow tie-dyes full of sights and sounds. My senses, for those 15 hours, were on overload. I understood very few words, as I consumed food and beverage. Their warmth, hospitality and smiles spoke volumes. Woman, men, children, families, my new *banjar*, embraced me as their own. I took pictures with so many people and children who were enthralled with the digital camera technology. To see themselves on a screen, seconds after a picture was taken, proclaimed a miracle in their eyes. My sticky rice was still in place.

With the moon at its highest peak, *Made* directed me towards the third temple's entrance. The orchestra resounded, leading a sacred parade of dancers flowing in our direction. Their destination was the entrance of the third temple. It was the closing ceremonies. I cried and snapped as many pictures as I could through my blurry, soaked eyes.

The third temple contained endless statues of Gods and Balinese folklore. Incense burned and offerings filled the Balinese dawn. The dust, kicked up from the barefooted dancers, didn't taste like dirt. The dancers entered the temple. Each stood, kneeled and bowed in individualistic harmony. Formal temple clothes and mother earth's ingredients married each other. Chants and songs of praise resounded. Made took me to the entrance of the temple; but we were not permitted into the ceremony. I was instructed that pictures were not permitted due to the level of sacredness of their individual and collective journeys. Silence filled the village of Sanur, Bali air; as priests began their honored and earned religious ritualistic rites. I felt like Mike Wallace, of the TV show 20/20, on location and reporting live. Men and women went into trances; as their heightened sacred enlightenment ignited human physical contortion and change. Physical and spirited movements, coupled with rolling eyes and flailing joints, were witnessed. I was not scared.

Rather, I was filled with the excitement and ecstasy of another person reaching their spiritual nirvana. I was happy for them. They had no reason to be faking. There were no cameras rolling or egos to be stroked. They opened their hearts and minds to the essence and outcomes of religious dedications.

I believed.

I made my way back to the hotel room, continuously thanking *Made* for a once in a lifetime experience. I exited his car saying goodbye and strolled through the garden pathways of my hotel, *Inna Sindhu Beach Hotel*. I don't think my feet hit the ground. Upon me, I felt an aura never experienced or acknowledged. I knew this trip would change me; because I wanted it too. However, from that ceremony, I would never be the same again. I reveled in that new reality which contained ingredients of the person I wanted to become.

I collapsed on my bed inside my hotel room; still dressed in the formal Balinese Hindu clothes that *Made* had given to me as a memory and keepsake of his appreciation for my enthusiasm, inclusion and participation. As slept crept in very slowly, I received a phone call from my brother back in the states. He was the family member communicating with me and sending out updated emails to family. With my eyes shut, barely awake, I was filled with endless gratitude for him introducing me to *Made*. I recounted my experiences of celebrating the Full Moon Festival. I can recount that ceremony, without hesitation, today and every day of my life. Sleep bestowed itself upon me. A volcano was in my future.

CHAPTER 12

The Mount Batur Sunrise

A van approached my hotel, under the 2am starry skies of the village of Sanur. A new moon's beams cut through the darkness brightly and seamlessly. The sky radiated a harvest moon, a bright moonlight that extended hours on the farms; providing more visual potential to reap the gifts of farmers' crops. I, on the other hand, was trekking the second largest volcano in Bali, *Mt. Batur*, to await the fall of the new moon and witness the sun come up over the island. My future lay before me in the gifts of experience, rather than crops.

We drove for a few hours, picking up passengers from all over the world, eventually parking in a small village. We disembarked and organized. Equipped with padded gloves and flashlight, I followed our tour guides across barren fields, towards the dark face of the beautiful volcano. In my previous excursions to the temples, I had already seen the volcano in daylight. My ongoing anticipation of experiencing this volcano firsthand was now over.

As we went around volcanic ash and debris, my Indonesian Sherpa pointed out that we were avoiding remnants of the last major eruption of Mt. Batur. To locals, this was still very prevalent in substance and memory. Asthma and my exhaustion from the previous night's Full Moon festivities hindered my pace. The guides were monumentally kind in their assistance leading me around jagged volcanic rocks and ledges. Towards the higher elevation of the volcanoes and mountains represented the Gods and I almost needed a God to finish this trek. The new moon, Hinduism, sobriety and perseverance were my fuel. Nothing was going to stop me.

Upon arriving at the top, there were a few scattered groups of people awaiting the same glorious vision of the morning breathing new life, awakening the day. It was still dark and recuperation, rather than socializing, took precedence.

My guide took me to the edge of the volcano and pointed down. I saw over a hundred beams of flashlights, coming from all directions. Small villages, surrounding the volcano, were spewing out fellow trekkers. They were people on the same journey with a thirst for experiential education. Each new person arrived on the peak, from different parts of the world, shared an unspoken enthusiasm for the same enrichment. We had mutually achieved the massive climb. Together, we simultaneously awaited our gifts from mother earth.

The top of the volcano contained remnants of a temple that reminded me of a major league baseball dugout. It was complete with a bench for sitting and a wall to lean back. The on-deck circle was the pinnacle of the volcano. The bathroom facility was literally a hole in the ground. Everyone embraced each other and united in the experience of mutual anticipation and conquest. I met people from all over the world, on top of Mt. Batur, sharing a common curious euphoria. I heard 10 different languages, all resounding with the same tone of pleasure and achievement. Emotions come in one language. Words can depreciate the gift of human experience.

Brill arriving on the peak for sunrise tour at Mt Batur volcanoe

As the sun rose and started burning of the heavy clouds and fog, I stood over the *calder*, the volcanic opening, wondering why this was happening to me. I still doubted my inclusion to experience such an event.

Such beauty should never be misinterpreted. It's universal and worthy for everyone. My tears filled the crater, dropping off my cheeks, into the unknown depths of darkness. Life wrapped its arms around me and simultaneously welcomed and bid farewell to each plummeted tear.

Tears of joy tumble differently.

I looked around at couples hugging and kissing; friends' arms draped over each other. I realized I was alone. It stung. It is at these travel moments, I often wish I could share this moment with someone, anyone. My Sherpa came over and hugged me. He said, "Ketut, Mike, you like?" ....

I didn't have to say a word, my smile and tears said it all.
I hugged him tightly, realizing I'm never alone.
Alone is a creation of self,
in a mind that wants to steal away the positive potential of experience.
My Mom and Dad were there. Everyone I
wanted to be there was with me.
I began hugging strangers.

As I descended from the volcano, new visions came to life, breathing a new world, which was not perceivable, to the human eye, during a dark 3am assent. From the beginning of the trek downward, as my eyes turned away from the magical sunrise and panoramic views of the entire island of Bali, I realized we were going back down towards the remains of the most recent eruption of Mt. Batur in 2000. Here I was 7 years later, on top of a volcano that recently erupted, enjoying every second, and I would soon be walking back down by the memories of horror and devastation for the citizens surrounding the volcano. My energy steered empathetically for the victims.

Descending, I felt a compassionate sadness, realizing the fullest negative ramifications of an active volcano. Those emotions were consoled with the emerging view of the peaceful waters of Lake Batur. Mt. Batur is the female volcano in Bali, while Mt. Agung, the larger of the two, is the male volcano. The new sites and visions of Mt. Batur, on the morning trek downward, presented waters, landscape and archeological wonders. Old temples and home remnants were still intact with breaths of life still resounding. To the locals, it was a reminder of the future catastrophic possibilities. I hoped the Gods would protect me on my journey of sobriety, while selflessly praying for the Balinese people's safety in the coming years. On this trip, the Balinese became my family.

In Bali, I visited countless temples. Each contributing a unique understanding of Hinduism and the power of a collective society. The Goa Lawah Temple "Bat Temple" was built in the 11th century, surrounds a bat cave. During the day, as I walked around the grounds, I could hear thousands of bats echoing from the dark cave. At dusk, they woke and flew out of the cave, fulfilling their nocturnal missions and scaring the shit out of me.

My visit to the largest temple in Bali, *Besakih Temple*, stood three thousand feet up the 9,944-foot face of the largest volcano, Mt. Agung. After being let off the bus, I walked straight up a "San Francisco" style steep road. To each side were artisans and market stands selling everything imaginable. As I approached the entrance of the temple, its magnificence came into perspective. The temple appeared to be endless. In layers, it just kept rising up the face of the volcano into the clouds. Each layer contained different portions of the temple.

I visited the Tanah Lot Temple, which is only accessible during low tide. During high tide the temple becomes an island. From various pictures taken at a distance, the island temple resembles a sinking ship.

During my visit to the artisan town of *Ubud*, I witnessed live and firsthand the awesome talents and output of every type of artist using every raw material available on the island. The woodwork and statues were majestic. During lunch in *Ubud*, I finished reading Elizabeth Gilbert's book, *Eat, Pray and Love.* I realized I was reading her portion of the book when she was in *Ubud*, Bali. I finished her book in the town in Bali that she visited on her amazing 3 country trek. By the way, her book is not a "chick book," as some men have alluded to. I highly recommend this read for all human beings, searching to improve themselves. When my bus was leaving to return to the hotel, I bid them farewell. I wasn't done with *Ubud*. I found a room and stayed the night. I returned to my hotel the next day, more alive and fulfilled, having ceased the day and the village of *Ubud* a little longer.

Serendipitously, at my hotel, they hosted a holistic conference, which all residents were permitted to attend. I participated in Asian yoga/exercise, meditation and massage workshops.

On one of my final days, I golfed at *Nirvana Golf Club*. I rented clubs and embarked on 18 holes of pure blissful golfing. Twelve of the holes were along the Indian Ocean. One fairway contained an actual Hindu Temple's remnants. I had to hit shots around the temple, but stopped in paused and said a prayer. I don't remember my score that day, as it didn't matter. The views and company of a fellow American and father and son team made a memorable foursome.

Brill golfing at Nirvana Golf Club with Tannah Lot Temple in Background

I can still smell Bali. Forever, in my heart and mind, it truly was my time of pure maturation and spiritual development. The people, religion, paradise and culture changed me every way fathomable. I will never be the same again. *Terima Kasih* (thank you) and *kedamaian* (peace), Bali.

CHAPTER 13

The Biggest Step Forward
Is Going Back

I have traveled all over the world. Each journey has countless contributions of experiential education formulating my spiritual development. I've come to believe everything is spiritual. Everything has meaning and purpose; and meaning and purpose is spirituality.

I've been to England, France, Ireland (3 times), Greece, Indonesia, Mexico, Caribbean and 21 states in America. The journey inward, through these external trips and spiritual transformation, has been a struggle, but consistently contains a goal of accomplished enlightenment. This holistic enlightenment reality requires ongoing attention, revision and inclusion. As my brother peacefully advised on the day I went into treatment: *open heart and open mind, letting people in to help.*

As an active alcoholic, I was incapable of positive outcomes. My progression of addiction proved this reality, through my ongoing failures from poor decision-making models. I came to believe I was a failure, often times sabotaging my life and opportunities of success to confirm that label. After being up from a binge, there were times I looked out the window and laughed at the people going to work, living a "normal" life. My view of the world was negative. But when things got really bad, spiraling, I looked out the same window, viewed the same people participating and contributing to their lives, and said "I could never do that." The saddest progression of addictions and most detrimental was my negative view of self, ignoring my positive potential.

I've heard of some research confirming the gene for addictions exists. To be honest, I'm not sure of this being confirmed. What has been confirmed over years of research and confirmed by the government is that addiction is a disease. My disease of addiction which developed over time is neurological, but often perceived by self and others as selfishness and low self-esteem. This is what most people see and experience. This developed opinion, through others' reality experienced firsthand, gives birth and ongoing confirmation, by many people, that addiction is not a disease. Rather, unfortunately, many people see it as a moral failing. This debate will continue forever. But keep in mind, as this moral-failing model trumps the disease model, self-esteem and empowerment of the active addict decreases, while negative stigmas and stereotypes increase. Furthermore, access to holistic treatment decreases.

Today, the reality of increasing numbers of people knowing an addict or alcoholic is becoming more common and spoken about than in generations prior. Almost everyone knows someone. The degrees of separation from an addict or alcoholic are thinning. It is no longer my father's, brother's, nephew's college roommate. It is sons and daughters; mothers and fathers; brothers and sisters. Today, most people are on the front lines, experiencing, firsthand, the negative ramifications of addiction. The severest outcome of death is a daily statistical news headline. Those people, along with the active addict or alcoholic, need spiritual enlightenment. The foundation of this enlightenment comes through an explanation, not a derogatory label of moral failure.

The disease model is that explanation (not an excuse), which is necessary for the acceptance and early healing of all people involved. I've perceived in my professional counseling experience, the correlation is that as firsthand, primary experience and stress of dealing with an addict goes up, so too does the acceptance of the disease model. Human beings can benefit from an explanation in order to initiate efforts in healing. Integrated with faith, these two aspects can initiate quality efforts towards recovery for everyone involved.

I walked into treatment thinking I was dropped off from Mars. I thought: Why couldn't I be like others, why am I different, even in my own family? The disease model explanation, not the excuse, was soothing, motivational and the cement foundation to understanding me and my addiction.

Moving forward becoming involved in participating in my life and recovery, a reaping and dedication to already existent experiences and energy became my Higher Power. These core beliefs, spiritual principles, ethics or whatever a person chooses to call it, began to dissipate my own righteous ignorance because now I was basing all my decisions on something outside of myself. My righteous ignorance was born in thinking in the scope of being right or wrong, moral fibers. Eventually, this righteous ignorance told me I could achieve nothing, because I could not do anything right. Untreated addiction confirms this consistently.

Everyone needs a program of living. During my infantile stages of sober recovery and spiritual development, I was provided the directional and creative freedom, through a suggestion, to construct personal beliefs and ultimately my own dedication to Higher Power(s). Immediately, I felt empowered from this chore. I am powerless when the substance is in me. Through abstinence from the substance, immediately recovery gave me the opportunity of power and freedom through the responsibility of creating and tapping that energy of a Higher Power.

Human empowerment, through choice, increases self-esteem. Sobriety, spiritual development or anything in life starts with a choice. I choose a broad, solitary goal. The goal was a better life. Spiritual development would bring me to this new life.

Tabula Rasa, a blank slate, needed to become a reality and the starting point in my new life. I needed to humble myself and literally admit to knowing nothing. My last 6 ½ years proved that I could not make productive decisions, thus change and manage my life. Now, if perceived and done productively, the worst 6 ½ years of my life, then became an asset.

As I moved along in my learning development, I sprinkled in my numerous past experiences, character traits and lessons that stood as ignored assets in my life. Eventually, I would manage the heavy liabilities. My focus needed to become the reaping of fruitful knowledge and wisdom that would soon become *Brillism*, my personal constructed spirituality. I became a student and my own historian.

It started with a choice born out of willingness. My willingness and efforts began by tapping the energy of my parent's life and what they provided as my parents and human beings. Quotes from the Dalia Lama, parables from the Bible or what my college professor told me after my final are sources of energy already real and produced. I exert energy to remember and synthesize those real contributions to life. Therefore, my Higher Power became energy. Every keg of beer I tapped, I got beer out of it. Every time I pause to tap these past positive assets and experiences in my life, I get positive outcomes. This keeps it simple for me.

On a daily basis, I have the responsible choice to honor or deny the plentiful and fruitful Higher Powers that exist and I have acknowledged throughout my life and recovery. These sources of enlightenment have always existed. However, now my choice is to synthesize them and make them a part of my daily decisions to improve my life and the world around me. Humility surfaces when I accept that I was once not able to achieve this task. Empowerment and positive self esteem occurs when you take a suggestion to create the dedication to a power and put a demand on your life to nurture and honor this creation. This is the core of human responsibility.

The only requirement was that this source of power(s) had to be greater than me. That is also humility. In my opinion, at the end of my addiction and in early recovery, I thought everything and everyone was greater than me. I could fill a notebook with derogatory adjective terms related to myself and my lifestyle in addictions. In my addiction, I considered myself a piece of shit.

Through this ongoing fluid and honest commitment to a power or energy, my powerlessness decreased because the process of healing and creating a Higher Power, in return, provided me with the power. My powerless only existed during the use of substances. I am always powerless over the substance, but only if they are consumed. Drinking alcohol and using drugs is always an option. It is never off the table. In the decision to not use or drink and keeping it always an option, I find my greatest victory and reward in choosing and exerting energy towards abstinence with purpose and meaning.

I did not drink or use drugs one day at a time and my life got better. I put in the work and my life improved exponentially. Selectivity does not exist in surrender and acceptance of my addiction. Surrender and acceptance are absolutes. I don't simply surrender during the winter months or on weekends. I need to surrender outright every day. Acceptance cannot be fragmented either. Acceptance is by the whole or nothing. I accepted who and what I was, an addict and alcoholic, and I surrendered to developing a better way of life – ABSOLUTELY! I became a Face and Voice of Long Term Sobriety.

On a steamy summer day in 2003, during my first year of sobriety, I took the suggestion of visiting my friend, Tom. He had already provided the suggestion of swimming in the freedom of choice for my Masters programs and I thirsted for more productive suggestions and directions from him. I took the bus to his house and remember wondering how I was going to proceed with my spirituality. At this time, I accepted my disease of addiction and believed in spirituality as a pathway of recovery. I had already formed a belief in people, parents, God and anything of substance that would equate and amount to a power greater than myself that would help me make healthier decisions. The power was increasing qualitatively and quantitatively. But still, I fought, doubted and faced challenges. The challenges in self-doubt were also my creations or a lower power at work. The plan of commitment, stemming from my creation of spirituality, occurred when we sat in his apartment and read to each other.

It is typically an awkward situation when two men are alone, reading to one another. But remember, I accepted and surrendered to a pathway of healing. We paused during the reading, to collaborate and learn more about the information provided. We each had input and were mutually benefiting from the other's experience and opinion. At one point, we decided to pray. This was the moment when my creative belief, needed an ingredient of action. The words, forming sentences, that sometimes people refer to as prayer, steered me towards not just believing. Rather, it steered me towards the empowerment of realizing my thoughts, emotions and behaviors should be aligned with goodness. The prayer, chanting or whatever you want to label it, worked for me that day.

From surrendering, I was winning.

The experienced opportunity of opening my heart and mind to this process and presently committing to a spiritual connection changed my life forever. I rarely tell this story, in fear of being ridiculed or locked up for insanity. Most ears receiving this tale have been in recovery. I feel those are the people that would understand the most. As Tom and I knelt in reverence and recited the prayer, something began happening to the living room. More specifically, it occurred through my vision. Furniture or other physical objects didn't begin to fly around the room. My eyesight became riddled with tiny balls of color. Close your eyes tight and focus. What do you see? That is what happened to my vision with my eyes wide opened. Pun intended. The room became a dance hall for this multitude of colorful bouncing balls. I became warm. I shivered through the change of core body temperature. I wasn't done.

We smiled afterwards and I said nothing about my profound experience. I had to gather my thoughts before murmuring this to anyone, not even the person whom I just shared the moment. I gathered my things, bid my farewell and walked towards the bus.

As I was leaving my friend's apartment, my steps became heavy and hesitant. My logistics of where I was going and what time and day it was became obscure. All simple facts and knowledge left me. I struggled for each step forward. I struggled through three steps and became exhausted. I stopped. Push, breath, breath, push. Was I giving birth? I certainly was giving "birth" and my slate was cleared, *Tabula Rasa*, a blank slate, became a newly born reality. I opened myself and let what was happening procced through me. I gave it permission to become a reality in my life. I then provided and empowered myself with the permission to start again – my second chance at life.

Each day provides humans the capabilities to start again and/or finish the tasks of yesterday. These are vital strategic opportunities to becoming a better, fuller human being. We can declare a starting line, at any point of time in our life. Today is all we got and throughout the day we can start, redo or resume any aspect of life. It all sounds like a cliché. Well it is. Or it is whatever you want to call it.

Labels and spirituality are subjective. On that day, through two friends mutually opening their hearts to enlightenment, I received the grace to become a spiritual individual. The calendar was brand new. Time was on my side. In the parking lot of my friend's apartment, I walked through a door of spiritual opportunity. I can close it whenever I want. I don't ever want to. I simply opened up my heart and mind to something new and become willing as only the dying can be. Through once dying, I want to live now.

My desperation became a gift when it drove me to change.

CHAPTER 14

March Forth

Immediately after the euphoric revelation through the permission of starting my life again; as a responsible spiritual sober person, I needed to open up Pandora's Box. My dark past needed to be brought to the surface and put into the light of truth. I could only do this as a new, powerful spiritual man.

I would spend about 7 weeks exploring negative past realities, toxic emotions and unproductive behaviors. I needed to take honest accountability for what I did wrong; manage the permanent traumas and heavy experiences in my life; while relinquishing my resentments of all people and situations. These harsh past realities were like cinder blocks tied to my ankle while swimming in a lake. They would eventually take me under and kill me. Worst of all, they were the quintessential ingredients to every excuse I created to drink and use drugs. The light was calling despite my fear of revealing and dealing with the truth.

Luckily, I remembered what I had previously done to arm myself with a power through spiritual development. After engaging proactively in my spiritual practices, over four weeks, knowing that I could not fly solo on this exploration and mange my life, I finally called my friend, Tom. He was happy I was working hard on this process. He eventually told me to now open up my ears, listen with my heart, and try to relate to others' experiences. Discouraged, I did exactly what he said. After two weeks of this process of open listening, I added more pertinent material. While I found a path of empathy to other people's negative experiences, it was other people's sharing of parallel experiences that aided me in remembering and facing my past. I added these treasured reminders with trembling hands.

This "skeletons from the closet" process can be the most daunting for any human, but especially someone in early recovery. It is a battle between past challenging the present, with the goal of building self-esteem. From personal and professional experiences, I have witnessed this process take many people out of recovery. Their spiritual connection is ignored and soon there becomes a reliance on self-will, rooted in low self-esteem that leads to relapse.

The process asks a recovering person to reflect on their entire life history of unproductive realities. This darkness should be brought into the light. Trauma should be an honest focal point. Most people refer to this process as emptying the waste basket. However, I have never seen a piece of trash again, after it was disposed of properly. The past is permanent, not discarded. Its real truth and chore are to be managed in order for life and sobriety to be sustained qualitatively.

These truths and realities of the past are often fear provoking and heavy weights that have drained a human being from their existence. Addictions and the past's horrid living outcome consists of low self-esteem and deprecating thoughts that have imprisoned the person.

In my addictions, I viewed myself as a piece of shit that wanted to die every day. Waking in hospitals and two suicide attempts reinforced this self-conceptualization. The surfacing of these realisms creates a Pandora's Box effect by engaging and contrasting an individual's years of efforts and failsafe strategies to suppress these life burdens for their own protection. I tried to manage my past unsuccessfully, with the outcome being the consumption of illicit substances.

The substances were only a symptom of my disease. If Snapple and Slim Jims got me high and --numb, I would have robbed every WaWa and 7-11's, convenient stores, of their stock. If I chased substances in addictions, why would I give them attention in recovery. In treatment, during one of my men's therapy groups, I brought up the idea that I could play music and drink O'Doul's, a non-alcohol beer. The debate roared on with my peers and the old lady, facilitating this weekend men's group, sat back professionally without saying a word and let the process proceed. After

20 minutes, she finally opened her mouth and asked me a question that saved my life. She asked:

"Michael, why would you want to consume something, that reflects the substance that wants you dead?"

Most human beings, in early recovery, do not have the coping skills to face these heavy past realities. A person with long term addiction, often rooted in trauma, avoids this process of coping as a cautionary process of preserving a semblance of the abnormal being normal. It becomes a safe, comfort zone. After years of this tactic anything repeated unsuccessfully would become normal to anyone. Diets often depress people, as the failures can bring on a question of self-worth or potential.

My personal and professional opinion is that most people, at this point in recovery, could benefit from professional clinical assistance, during this process, to secure a positive self-view, along with a stronger commitment to their personal spirituality. I call it *Asset Retrieval.*

My capability and commitment to spiritual development directly correlates to my efforts and outcomes of managing my negative past. I proved that I was incapable of such a process and positive outcome. As noted earlier, my capability to open my heart and mind up to a belief and commitment to a Higher Power gave way to physical and mental occurrences of a colorful living room that would have me questioned by most people. People in recovery understand me and my narrative of this unforgettable and awesome miracle. With my Higher Power and recovery in each hand and fully implanted in my heart, I felt unstoppable. There's power for you.

After engaging a positive motivation with attainable goals towards positive self-esteem related to this process, I began reflecting on my dark past. Fearlessness and honesty were vital. Dishonesty and omission cause relapse. I had to embark on this course of action in a spiritual manner, remembering I am in the process of change. My way didn't work and my pathway of addictions proved this to me.

After a few weeks of embarking on this vigorous endeavor, I called my Tom to tell him I was ready to discuss my past. He was happy to hear of my efforts but quickly suggested I open my ears and heart, continuing on my exploration. A few weeks later, my friend provided me the same suggestion. Each time I heard his suggestion I became angry. On my terms,

I was ready. Inside this process was emotional management. I was dealing with raw opened wounds of the past. He was correct in suggesting there could be more material that could be lodged from my subconscious past irretrievable by my own efforts. Through listening to other sober people sharing their own experiences, my own similar past scenarios surfaced. No matter how big or how small the situation, if it reflected my dark past, I added it to my personal list. I was creating a past reality check. At times I didn't know that person nor did I want to admit it was me.

After my third phone call to Tom, while expecting to hear the same suggestion, he provided me with a date and time for us to meet to discuss my past. I was unable to singlehandedly and masterfully commend my past. Its manageability alone would take years of practice. But on this day, I was to rely on a friend, sober support, to bring my past into the light. It was a trifecta, consisting of myself, a friend and spirituality. That morning in prayer I asked Mom and Dad to come along.

After arriving at my friend's apartment, I handed him my deep dark past on 4 pieces of paper. I was ready. He invited me to have some pizza and soda. I sat back, relaxed and he shared his honest life story of struggles and triumphs. This man that was guiding me in my development saved my life on that breezy fall day. Upon completing his story and even after all of his perfect suggestions of further listening and reflection in completing this process, my trauma box opened again and my world came tumbling down on me.

I immediately grabbed my horrific history back from him and my eyes filled with tears as my childhood pursuit for the Big Leagues surfaced. After my experience of dancing, colorful balls of light, *Tabula Rasa*, rekindling my relationship with my parents and ongoing spiritual development efforts, I was ready to carry the heaviest anchor of my life, denying the light of truth on my greatest darkness. Twenty-one years later, no one knew and I still didn't want people to know of my sexual abuse trauma. With pen in hand, I added the monster who sexually abused me, to my list.

On that day, I was free from its toxins.

My entire dark past was brought into the light. For years, I suppressed, ignored and mismanaged this trauma. Truthfully, I walked around with hate and anger in my heart. There were moments, knowing he was dead, that I wanted to dig up his grave and stab him in the eye a thousand times with a fork. He took my innocence and here I was, in early sobriety, ready to carry this pain with me for the rest of my life. Through my present engagement, healing and sobriety, I now believe my *Tears of Clown* phase began from my disassociation and suppression of my childhood sexual abuse trauma.

Although trauma is a tattoo in permanence, there is hope and it is manageable. Ultimately, it comes from within. I was not hypnotized that day in order to forget my darkness. Rather, I was instilled a responsibility, as the curator of my past, the freedom to live productively allowing myself to face this reality as a man of honor and dignity.

Trauma is like the game whack-a-mole. Trauma will return in many different forms and with varying intensities. If I believe in myself and trust my efforts in recovery and spirituality, I will always win. As a tool of healing, I began to pray for the monster's soul and all those effected by sexual abuse. My healing is in writing this book, hoping others share their story or do not become victims.

I could say I forgive him, but I would be lying. Forgiveness, like surrender and acceptance, is another one of life's absolutes. On most days, I do forgive that sick man who manipulated and made me do those horrible things. In some moments, while fixated on the scary moments, I don't forgive him, while wishing it never happened. On those days with those moments, I never shut my eyes in bed without praying and forgiving. I don't take blame anymore and I pray for the strength to someday forgive him completely. As the *Saw Doctors*, from Galway, Ireland sang:

> *Life's too short for wasting, for ifs and might have beens, and*
> *life's too short for wondering if you could have lived your dreams.*
> *And its way too short for loneliness and we don't have to be.*
> *Now that we trust each other, why don't you stay with me.*

Copyright 1997 Saw Doctors "Share the Darkness"

I lost so much of my life mismanaging emotions, hiding in my secret and deprecating thoughts related to the actual moments of my specific trauma. The lingering permanent essence of trauma will not defeat me. I am committed to my wellness and improving the world I live in. I have taken the reins of responsibility through the adoption and honoring a program of living along with professional counseling to revisit this trauma, which helps me "whack that fuckin mole" each time it pops up its rearing head.

CHAPTER 15

We Are Doing It Wrong

It is my duty to warn you that this chapter is mutually the most clinical and change initiative chapter in my book. It is my experience and voice as a professional, licensed counselor; working in addictions treatment and recovery. Also, while this entire book is special to me, this chapter I hope will provoke some advocacy for treatment, diagnosis and clinical interventions in the treatment for persons with substance use disorders.

I don't claim to have solutions, as many people and movements in the field would like to communicate. The term and reality of solution has been thrown around today by many organizations and movements, preying on a desperate population of people that have been directly affected by the epidemic of addictions. Also, follow the money trail and see who is offering those "solutions."

Opiods are not the epidemic. Trauma and relapse are the epidemic. Opiods, like Snapple and Slim Jims, are just a substance. In the 1980's, crack was the epidemic, presently it is opiods. In 5 years, our country will realize we've been ignoring a debilitating rise in crystal methamphetamine use, due to individuals engaging in alternative, cheaper drug usage. These substances should not be the focus of diagnosis and treatment in addictions recovery. A clinical, person-centered trauma pathway towards the solution of healing the human being should be developed. Again, trauma and relapse are the epidemic. Every addictions counselor should be certified in treating trauma and that should be the humanistic pathway and work of both counselor and client.

The problem and solution lay within every individual in treatment and recovery. I believe in multiple pathways of treatment and recovery. However, ultimately, the person in recovery is responsible for accountable behaviors and spiritual growth on a daily basis. The foundation of this healing is bringing trauma to the surface and guiding client's toward managing its ongoing resurgence through positive self-esteem building. This is my experience and my opinion stemming from professional and personal experience.

In one of my many attempts in finishing college and obtaining my Bachelor's Degree, I studied to be a High School History Teacher. Along with Education courses, high school teachers needed a concentration. Mine was my history. I had no idea how profound and useful the subject matter of the education courses would help me later in life and career in becoming a better counselor.

This third or fourth attempt at higher education occurred in the early to mid-1990's. I was attending LaSalle University in Philadelphia. Education in the United States of America was going through a drastic student-centered reformation. Education was being challenged on all levels. Therefore, the education and training of future teachers, on the college level, was diligent and militant in producing a positive change in national educational standards of achievement. Teaching, learning and testing of students were placed under the microscope. Around 1991, one man had the bravery to tell the United States of America that they were doing it (education) wrong. This example is strictly to make my point of facilitating change.

William Gardner of Harvard University examined cognitive development and learning in school age children. His studies revealed that classrooms were not productive in conforming to a student-centered philosophy of teaching. As classroom sizes were averaging 35 to 50 students in the 1990's, Gardner brought to life the reality that every student does not learn the same way. Moreover, testing in a solitary fashion does not give every student a fair chance at educational success.

Referring to testing or the process of giving back covered information at a certain period of time, signifying students' success or failure, he declared there is a lacking in tapping the individual students' assets. One student may learn from a lecture through taking notes, while another student would learn more from music, movie, handouts or a play. Students that are good at reading and comprehension may be lacking the ability to take productive notes and lack the reference skills to later prepare for a test.

Each student does not have the equal ability to regurgitate the information back to the teacher in a testing environment. While some students may have the ability to write an essay; other students would benefit from a test containing multiple choice and true or false questions. There are students that would excel at giving an oral presentation on WW II, while other students, if having to give the same presentation, would crawl into shell of anxiety. However, the same student in that shell could write a song or ever direct a play on WWII and achieve highly in grading satisfaction.

Educators were being challenged to accommodate each student by tapping their assets to achieve. In order to capture the full range of abilities and talents in the classroom, Gardner came up with a theory of multiple intelligences. Since the birth of this theory, classrooms have changed, schools have been created and the job of educators to acknowledge, motivate and prepare has made their jobs daunting and that much more challenging. Expectations married to new learning environments and pathways, in the classroom, gave way to better individual and collective educational opportunities.

I use this example as a facilitator and example of holistically challenging and changing a system and focusing on individual assets as means of learning and growing. Addiction treatment is doing it wrong and person-centered trauma treatment needs to occur more often.

Let's heal human beings, rather than making pharmaceutical companies richer.

After getting sober in 2003, I returned to college for the fifth time. My first job full time job in sobriety was at the Hospital of University of Pennsylvania (HUP). My cousin worked there and had asked me numerous times to come work there. Luckily, I never took her offer. My addictions and lifestyle would've had me burning that bridge in a few weeks. I was incapable of sustaining gainful employment. If a job paid me $10,000.00 a week, shortly after the first pay, I would have walked away from the job due to my addictions.

After a year of sobriety, with my welfare benefits running out, I began applying for more benefits. As I was filling out the application and getting advice from someone, I was instructed to provide false information. I erased my truthful answers in order to better my chances of continuing my welfare benefits. As I was completing the application, one of my crucial miracles of early sobriety happened.

I grew a conscience.

Sobriety, after one year, isn't about a drink or drug; rather, it's about seizing every moment and doing the right thing. A conscious comes with responsibility. Responsibility promotes citizenship. These are all endorsed and supported with every decision I make. I ripped up the application, picked up the phone and I called my cousin. I told her I was ready for work. Her response contained a condition that if she was going to get me the job I would need to go back to school and get my degree, through the job benefits. She did not have to twist my arm. I agreed.

After working as a temp for 10 months, then being hired full time, my benefits began after my first 90 days. On that 90th day, I went to LaSalle University for a credit evaluation procuring my enrollment. In that first attempt, while sober, I obtained my bachelor's degree in Sociology, Education and History. I received a General Education BA, which required a major and two concentrations to fulfill its requirement. In a hidden blessing, only becoming a glaring reality during enrollment, this degree attainment was only possible from all my educational attempts and ample changes of declared majors, over the years. In 2007, I finally graduated.

Unbeknownst to my cousin, in my final semester of undergraduate studies, I began applying for Graduate School. After fulfilling my obligation and her contingency of employment, I was accepted into two graduate programs. I remember the day I walked into her office and presented her with the letters of acceptance. We both cried.

After 4 grueling years of full-time work, part time school and 700 hours of internships (sometimes 80-hour weeks with adding study hours), I graduated from Holy Family University with a Master's of Science in Counseling Psychology and a concentration in Student Affairs (working with the college population in higher education).

After 7 years of employment, as an Insurance Research Clerk at HUP, I began my first career. I was 41 years old and 8 years sober. I started a job at a career school, as a Career and Student Services Advisor. While I was trained to work with the post high school population, the job did not focus on clinical counseling as much as I preferred.

After two years, I got a job at Self Help Movement Inc., a men's substance use disorder residential treatment center in Northeast Philadelphia. I have worked there for 6 years. I have attained the credentials of LPC (Licensed Professional Counselor in Pennsylvania), NCC (Board Certified-National Certified Counselor), and CCTP (Certified Clinical Trauma Professional).

Self Help Movement Inc, in Northeast Philadelphia, is a successful rehabilitation center, with higher than national average success rates. It provides an opportunity, if approved by insurance, to go through two levels of care. Inpatient and Halfway House Levels of Care provide men the chance to be in treatment for almost 5 months. In the Halfway House, men live in a structured, peer-driven and clinical environment, while permitted out in the community to develop their citizenship and recovery skills. Access to this type of long-term and accountable treatment needs to be available to everyone, through all insurances.

The title of this chapter or more specifically the "We" is referred to the system or industry of diagnostic driven treatment. Our facility is not a dual diagnosed institution. As a licensed clinician, I am qualified to diagnosis across all behavioral and mental criteria. However, working in this facility does not permit me to do so. Clients' primary diagnosis in our facility pertains to the substance disorder and the severity level. We have a contracted part time psychiatrist that we refer clients to if there is a mild to moderate history or present reported diagnosis from detox or previous treatment. The psychiatrist is on staff as well for the continuance of clients' psychotropic medication schedules and follow up.

My personal sobriety does not qualify me for my counseling job. Furthermore, my career is not my program of sobriety. I must work for my sobriety by engaging in the program of recovery I have adopted and practice in the community, starting the day I left treatment. However, both career and personal recovery have provided me great insight into the real and clinical aspects of helping human beings with substance use disorders.

I use the phrase, substance use disorders, loosely. Over the years the Diagnostic Statistics Manuel (DSM), used for diagnosing, has been updated 5 times. The DSM has been widely criticized and argued by professional and patients. Many clinical professionals in private practice would prefer not using the DSM and choose not to, preferring cash payment over insurance reimbursement. However, the driving entity of the insurance industry and the almighty dollar keeps the DSM in place as the primary source of referrals and payments for maladies pertaining to behavioral health.

The massive recovery and treatment advocacy movement in the United States, pertaining to substance-use disorders, has facilitated many successful outcomes, pertaining to decreasing the stigmatization and discrimination of people suffering from alcoholism and addictions. The first diagnosis of Alcoholism and Drug Dependence appeared in the 1952 DSM II. Since that time, over the course of 3 more versions, the advocators have been able to minimize the harm ratio through changing the language used in this type of diagnosis. Dependence, abuse, habitual, intoxication, and physiological have given way to the less intensive and discriminatory phrasing; thus the present Substance Use Disorder.

Clients being treated for substance use disorders receive a specific substance(s) i.e. marijuana, cocaine, opioids, etc and a severity level of mild, moderate and severe diagnosis. There are diagnostic qualifiers such as; the longevity, frequency and amount of substance being used that designates the severity. Since the diagnostic language that is being used is on a continuum of harmful reduction by advocacy movements, on behalf of the client, my question through personal and professional practice and observation, is why don't we get rid of the substance use diagnosis. Other than medical stability and health purposes, these diagnoses give too much emphasis and focus of treatment services and efforts on the substance. The individual's trauma needs to take precedent.

Through my professional work as a Counselor at a substance disorder facility and in my private practice, I am estimating 85-90% of my clients have experienced some level and type of trauma before their addiction emerged and became problematic. More often than not, this trauma is untreated, stagnating in suppression. This untreated trauma, compounded with an addictive progression and lifestyle which is also trauma riddled, is purely evident in the concrete and conscious views that a patient has of self and the world. It is purely distorted and unproductive.

If a client comes to me with a diagnosis of anxiety, I do not explore the specifics of the client's nail biting. Nail biting is only a symptom of the malady. Of course, the physical, medical safety of the client is explored, but more importantly the focus should be on the mitigating circumstances initiating the anxiety and the treatment plan for behavior and cognitive modification. Substance use disorder diagnosis focuses only on the substances: when, how much, frequency, last time and first time of usage. During the intake and initial clinical meeting performing a biopsychosocial, more time is spent on the substances than any other topic or source of information provided by the client.

I was homeless at the end of my addiction and between friends' couches, the occasional porch or shed. I lived in Pennypack Park in Northeast Philadelphia. I literally became content with that lifestyle. I felt I had arrived. I accepted this as my reality. This reality and concept are distortions for any human being.

Each day, to further my deprecating self-view, I would walk up the park's hilly dirt road that brought me out to the streets and world. Each time, I had one thought, that today would be the day I would get myself together, get help and make better decisions. I believed I'd turn the corner and everything would be a bed of roses or peaches and cream.

The insanity of this thought is engrained in the notion that I would get something from nothing. It was only a thought without proper action taken. Each morning, I ended up in the local corner bar, drinking with the third shift factory workers; as if I knew them my whole life. If I got there early enough, I could clean a floor or scrub a bathroom for free pints of beer. I ignored my thought or prospect of change and did nothing to make it happen rewardingly. Through all my past failures and ongoing creation of a hopeless reality, I subconsciously thought I was not worthy or capable of change, let alone a successful outcome. My view of self was damaging.

Trauma comes in many different forms. Childhood parental or self-divorce, death of loved ones, molestation/sexual abuse, neglect, prostitution, bullying, discrimination, segregation, military/war, witness to abuse, incarceration, institutionalization, witness or victim of crime, or victim of disasters can paralyze a human being. These are alive and real in most clients that are simply living in untreated trauma. The substances simply numb the pain they are experiencing.

PTSD became prevalent and a frequented diagnosis for soldiers returning from war. With no disrespect to all members of the branches of military, if you lived through an addiction you can easily refer to that diabolical progression as a war. The life of an addict is at-risk each day. The outcome of addictions, again, is a poor self-image and disconnection from the world.

Treating substance use disorders needs to go through a challenging human transformation. It is crucial to focus on person centered therapies that empower the client to construct a new narrative of their life by intensely examining trauma. These narratives need to be rooted in positive self-esteem and a realistic relationship with the world. The responsibility, solution and acknowledgement of both positive and negative outcomes have to emerge from the one suffering. From their construction comes their responsibility. Behavioral health professionals need to steer and tap the core values, motivations and assets of the client. As noted, the development of power through spiritual development is often beneficial.

In my professional development and practice modality, I immediately begin building positive esteem in clients. As a counselor, I tell my clients during the first session, that if I work more or less than 50% than I'm not doing my job. I encourage and empower the client, by making a pact, that each of us works 50%, in order to create the optimal outcome – 100%.

People often ask me how I build self-esteem in clients. My sarcastic answer is that I have clients do "esteem-able" things. My clinical answer is that I encourage and motivate the client to start living consciously by raising awareness to positive decisions they make, rooted in change. In my rehab facility, the front door is unlocked. Clients can choose to leave treatment whenever they so choose. Staff would attempt to retain the client and help them make a better decision. But ultimately it is up to the clients and their freedom and power of choice. I ask clients to be aware of this each time they pass by the door to go to their rooms or attend counseling sessions. Each time passing that front door is an achievement or goal attained in their personal decision and should be acknowledged by the person in treatment.

In early treatment, most clients want to leave every second of every day, due to the disease of addiction being recent and rampant; the lure of the drug or most often from the client not believing they can succeed in treatment or recovery.

After 6 weeks of inpatient treatment, I met with a client for the final time before stepping him down to our Halfway House Level of Care, located on our campus. He sat down in my office and he said "278." Baffled, I asked him what that meant. He explained: "since you asked me, I have walked by the front door 278 times during my inpatient stay." I fought back the tears, but more importantly I witnessed a smile on the client's face. He walked by the door. He counted. He acknowledged his achievements. He smiled. Simple conscious acknowledgments of achievements build positive self-regard and esteem.

I would wager a professional estimation that most clients, including myself, could and should be diagnosed with PTSD, with depression, anxiety and substance use disorders as symptoms or qualifiers of the PTSD primary diagnosis. Treat clients for PTSD, eliminate the discriminatory, degrading and symptomatic substances altogether.

Human beings are getting high just to get access to treatment. Loved ones, whose dream of having their loved ones finally ready for treatment, drive their family member or friend to obtain illegal narcotics so they have the substance in their system in order to gain access to treatment. This is Russian Roulette and is not acceptable.

As a CCTP (Certified Clinical Trauma Professional) along with other credentials and mandatory yearly trainings, I have sat through my certifications and trainings relating trauma to addictions. I shake my head each time wondering why this is not the focus of treatment. Educating clients towards understanding the addiction, relapse and other aspects of the disease is crucial and promotes peace through understanding. Knowledge is power. However, the individual focus should be on trauma.

In order to clarify and explain the PTSD diagnosis, as it is proclaimed in the *Diagnostic and Statistical Manual of Mental Disorders, 5th edition, 2013 (DSM-V)*, I will apply my own experience of childhood trauma of sexual abuse. If you are reading this book and suffered from trauma or addictions, apply your own experience and qualifiers to this example.

DISCLOSURE: This is only a tool of awareness and education. If you feel you have PTSD or symptoms please consult a behavioral

health specialist. If there are present severe symptoms or any type of emergency where you do not feel safe that arise from this reading, please go to the nearest trauma center or call 911.

There are 8 diagnostic criteria of PTSD in the DSM V. These criteria apply to adults, adolescents and children older than 6 years of age. I was approximately 12 years old at the time of my childhood sexual abuse trauma.

NOTE: The criteria that is bold, applies to my trauma experiential qualifier for diagnosis.

    A.   Exposure of actual or threatened death, serious injury or sexual violence <u>in one (or more) ways</u>:

        1.   **Directly experiencing the traumatic event**

        2.   Witnessing, in person, the event(s) as it occurred to others.

        3.   **Learning that the traumatic event(s) occurred to a close family member or close friend. In cases of actual or threatened death of a family member or friend, the event(s) must have been violent or accidental.**

        4.   Experiencing related or extreme exposure to aversive details of the traumatic event(s) (e.g., first responders collecting human remains; police offers repeatedly exposed to detail of child abuse)>

NOTE: For my diagnosis example, 2 of 4 criteria were present in A.

    B.   Presence of one (or more) of the following intrusion symptoms associated with the traumatic event(s), beginning after the trauma occurred.

        1.   **Recurrent, involuntary and intrusive distressing memories of the traumatic event(s)**

        2.   **Recurrent distressing dreams in which the content and/or affect of the dream are related to the traumatic event(s)**

        3.   **Dissociative reactions (eg. Flashbacks) in which the individual feels or acts as if the traumatic event(s) were recurring.**

4. **Intense or prolonged psychological distress at exposure to internal or external cues that symbolize or resemble an aspect of the traumatic event**

NOTE: For my diagnosis example; 4 of 4 criteria were present in B.

C. Persistent avoidance of stimuli associated with the traumatic event(s), beginning after the traumatic event(s) occurred, as evidenced by one or both of the following:

1. **Avoidance of or effort to avoid distressing memories, thoughts, or feelings about or closely associated with the traumatic event(s).**

2. **Avoidance of or efforts to avoid external reminders (people, places, conversations, activities, objects, situations) that arouse distressing memories, thoughts, or feelings about or closely associated with the traumatic event(s).**

NOTE: For my diagnosis example, both criteria were present in C.

D. Negative alterations in cognitions and mood associated with the traumatic event(s) beginning or worsening after the traumatic events(s) occurred, as evidence by two (or more) of the following:

1. **Inability to remember an important aspect of the traumatic event(s) (typically due to dissociative amnesia and not to other factors such as head injury, alcohol or drugs).**

2. **Persistent and exaggerated beliefs or expectations about oneself, others or the world (e.g. "I am bad," "No one can be trusted." "The world is completely dangerous." "My whole nervous system is completely ruined").**

3. **Persistent, distorted cognitions about the cause or consequences of the traumatic event(s) that lead the individual to blame himself/herself or others.**

4. **Persistent negative emotional state (e.g., fear, horror, anger, guilt, or shame).**

5. **Markedly diminished interest or participation in significant activities.**

6. **Feelings of detachment or estrangement from others.**

7. **Persistent inability to experience positive emotions (e.g., inability to experience happiness, satisfaction, or loving feelings).**

NOTE: For my diagnosis example, all 7 criteria were present in D

E. Marked alterations in arousal and reactivity associated with the traumatic event(s), beginning or worsening after the traumatic event(s) occurred, as evidenced by two (or more) of the following:

1. **Irritable behavior and angry outbursts (with little or no provocation) typically expressed as verbal or physical aggression toward people or objects.**
2. **Reckless or self-destructive behavior.**
3. **Hypervigilance**
4. **Exaggerated startle response**
5. **Problems with concentration**
6. **Sleep disturbances (e.g., difficulty falling or staying asleep or restless sleep)**

NOTE: For my diagnosis example, all 7 criteria were present in E.

F. **Duration of the disturbance (Criteria B, C, D, and E) is more than one month.**

G. **The disturbance causes clinically significant distress or impairment in social, occupational or other important areas of functioning.**

H. **The disturbance is not attributable to the physiological effects of a substance (e.g., medication, alcohol) or other medical condition.**

NOTE: For my diagnosis example, all of the last three criteria were present in F, G, and H).

My real example of my personal childhood traumatic experience of sexual abuse fits this diagnostic criterion. My addiction's progression and lifestyle also fulfill the criteria.

Again, it is crucial to understand that self-diagnostics is not recommended. My example of PTSD was simply to promote an arena of educating and raising awareness to PTSD's criteria. Please, consult an appropriate Counselor, Psychologist or Behavioral Health specialist, especially one certified in the treatment of trauma.

In the world of substance use disorder treatment and its recovery, the solution needs to be found and sustained from the person. It is crucial for sustaining and participating in long term sobriety and ongoing healing. The world has gone ahead and wrapped itself in bubble wrap. Humans in their present nature are delicate, to the point of avoidance of personal responsibility in fear it might cause them harm. A new narrative must be created by the person in order to live productively.

With the guidance and motivation from clinical counselors, a new narrative, rooted in truth, is possible. It is not an easy chore, often creating a feeling of back sliding. In the counseling process, reality gets worse before getting better. It's unavoidable, if healing is to take place. Opening up past wounds of trauma can be exhausting, producing every emotion humanly fathomable. That's where the hard work, by both client and counselor, becomes the most crucial.

Trauma treatment interventions, such as Prolonged Exposure, can take up to 16 weeks to process trauma with a certified professional. In substance use disorder treatment some patients struggle to get 28 days of treatment coverage from insurance companies. In this menial duration, counselors can only apply the best "band aid to the gunshot wound." If trauma was the primary diagnosis the duration of coverage should be longer in duration based on researched based interventions for trauma. It is long hard work by counselor and client, but a lifetime of awareness and hard work managing the trauma by the individual.

My uncle had an authentic human characteristic in compassionately making time for the young people in our family. I admire and cherish, to this day, his consistent interest in my life. He would make his way around family parties and weddings, find me and inquire about my life. He'd say: "How are you son?" After declaring my laundry list of young difficulties and challenges to him, my uncle would profoundly say to me "Well son, if it wasn't difficult, how great would the outcome be?"

CHAPTER 16

No Ifs, Ands With One B.U.T.

Sobriety or the greatest psychiatrist, psychologist or counselor does not remove or erase trauma. Neither do victims. My childhood sexual abuse; death of my parents within 8 months of each other; pathway of addictions; divorce and a recent medical crisis are permanent fixtures in my life. I listened, read, learned while being professionally counseled, in learning the tools from others to manage and understand these lingering and dark permanent realties.

Understanding, simply the word itself, brings peace to me. Its reality is awesome. The state of understanding than brings forth responsibility, while closing the door on excuses. Understanding is the permission note to an individual to create their new and productive living narrative. I lived in a world of excuses, during my addiction, and now my quest for contentment lies in the formation of factual explanations. I own my explanations today because I have constructed them. No more excuses.

Like a human needs air and a fish needs water, a sober person and trauma victims need to acknowledge and truly understand the past, present and future. There is no ifs, ands and only one "BUT" in life.

B.U.T.:

Believing in Tomorrow - **U**nderstanding Yesterday - **T**rusting Today

The avoidance and ignorance of B.U.T. is the truest human epidemic. It should be the ultimate procedural goal of counseling and human existence.

In my ignorant interpretation and analysis of my here and now realities, I avoided measuring and fully understanding everything in my life; both good and bad. Integral self-measurements are responsible emotional responses and analysis to stimuli. *How are you doing*? is a question that requires responsible and proactive measuring. Good and bad are polar-opposites and the typical response by most people.

If you think about polar-opposites, refer to the North Pole and the South Pole as the furthest points you can go on the earth. Those destinations, at the tip of the globe, are polar- opposites. What exists between these two measurements is the entire earth. Good and bad can be considered polar-opposites. Between good and bad, in humans, exists countless emotional realities that need acknowledgement, focus and familiarity.

It is an individual's responsibility to know what it looks like in their own life to be sad as opposed to depressed. Humans need to measure their anger and manage accordingly. Is the anger so severe that the person is going to hit and harm someone? Or is it causing an increased heart rate? These two realities create extremely different outcomes and consequences. Emotions and their measurements are subjective. One person's anger does not look or feel the same as in others. It is one's responsibility to learn about themselves on the measurement scale between the polarities. What lies between good and bad, happy and sad, angry and peaceful?

If the earth is 75% water, then we as humans are at least that statistic in emotions. If one wants to get to know themselves, then that person needs to solidify an awareness and responsibility to their personal emotions and ultimate responses.

During my second semester in my Master's program and during my Counseling Theories class, I was asked to write a paper, creating my own theory of counseling. My first thought was that all the ideas and theories were taken. My professor stimulated thought and creativity in me, towards creating my theory. He was successful in catching my attention.

My creation became *Simodelism*. Instead of using the prefix of "psy" used in psychology or psychiatrist, I used Simo. This prefix "Simo" refers to the first part of my theory, the game *Simon Says*. During the writing of this paper and throughout my counseling career, I have asked hundreds of people this question. "In the game Simon Says, how do you get to the next round in the game?" (PLEASE THINK ABOUT YOUR ANSWER NOW)

Ninety percent of the responses I received revolved around DOING what Simon says. This answer is only 50% correct. The other 50% of the correct answer is when a competitor in the game does nothing at the right time. When Simon doesn't say do it, you should do nothing to gain entry into the next round. If the participant performs the act when Simon didn't say, that person is eliminated.

The 90% responses of "doing" reflects are society in its state of habitual action. Immediate gratification and the world moving a mile a minute, with every answer at our finger tips, contribute to the avoidance or awareness that doing nothing is often beneficial, healthy and rewarding. Of course, human verbal response is to do something, while denying ourselves the luxury and freedom to do nothing and gain victory in our solitude of simply just existing. We, as humans, are victorious in our timing of doing something or nothing at the appropriate time.

The second part of my creative theory, *Simodelism*, refers to the second part of the word: *modelism*. Humility provides a human the opportunity and grace to admit that they are unable to do something. Or at least, do that something properly or to its fullest potential.

Modelism refers to the need for human beings to acquire lessons from others, role models. When I was little, I wanted to be Mike Schmidt or Jack Nicholas. Sure, they are great role models appropriate for lofty athletic goals. But Mike or Jack weren't there when I had my first job interview; or when it was time for my first kiss at Moss Playground's carnival. They certainly weren't there to help me manage trauma.

Behaviors, cognitions and social interactions are more frequently learned and mimicked. Core, human role models can be found in immediate, tangible and realistic members of our family, community or society. If I learned and applied one thing about work ethic from my father or brother, I would have been a better worker. If I learned from my other brother commitment to scholastics, I might not have gone to school for 19 years to get my bachelor's degree. My mother's kindness and grace would have had me dodge many arguments, confrontations and fist fights.

At the time, I thought I knew everything and remember I was always O.K. With real and authentic role models surrounding me, I denied myself their example and lessons. We, as humans, need to tap the skills and experiences of others in order to create our personal and stable decision-making model, rooted in cognitive, emotional and behavioral processing. Then, choosing when to do something or doing nothing is crucial for our existence.

I no longer compare my life to others. I've become positively infected by others. People by their simple example have consistently showed me with their example and existence, what to do and what not to do; how to be and how not to be. I've incorporated people as role models and inspirations. Internal practices, especially fueled in righteousness, have cursed me and led to unproductive behaviors, decisions and realities; even in my sober life. Presently, my life has many ingredients. As a responsible sober man, I am on a voyage of accountability through measurement, in the hopes of becoming a better man each day, while improving the world around me.

I feel I should tell you that I was not saved by Jesus, hypnotized or changed myself completely. One of my best friend's father once gave me the greatest compliment ever. It was in early sobriety and his words continue to grow exponentially. He said; "Brillo, you know what you did right in sobriety? You brought Mike Brill into your sobriety." This compliment continues to reinforce, even in my addiction, I was a good person. Parts of me were still intact by bringing the past assets of myself and marrying them to other role models influences into my role as a person in recovery. My developmental pathway was and continues to be the reaping and allocation of words and philosophies.

My spirituality is called *Brillism*. It's not cocky or selfish. Actually, it's the antithesis, representing attention, heightened awareness and synthesis of assets. I'm proud of it because it's my creation, slathered with donations from others. *Brillism* simply guides me in improving myself and the world. I don't want to recruit, hypnotize or trick anyone for my personal crusade in spiritual development. It's not a cult manipulation or exploitation of people's misfortune. It's mine and I want to always encourage, through word and example, others to develop their own.

I have constructed *Brillism* with pieces of religion, philosophy, parental advice, music, friendships, authors, quotes and movies; just to name a few. The list is endless and continues to grow with every conversation, reading, memory, interaction and experience. Spirituality does not lie during its acquirement. It is a form of reaping, where you take what is needed and leave the rest behind. Spirituality truly surfaces in people's lives when those resources and ingredients of beliefs and principles are applied to a life experience, relationship building, decision or dilemma.

Each day on Facebook, I see hundreds of posts containing inspirational quotes acquired from an online resource. These are wonderful beginnings to spiritual development. However, it is the application of these quotes to one's life scenarios that becomes the fruitful asset in people's lives and spiritual attainment.

Rarely does one single thing or process work autonomously. Spirituality needs allies. It has partners. It manifests. Life becomes a connect-the-dot-book, where people, events and efforts become a smattering of dots on a single page, called life. Those dots are the past and present assets acquired over time. I need to connect the dots to make the present beautiful picture come to life. I can't wait to color it in.

Responsible people do responsible things. Connecting the dots, or acknowledging the causes and effects of my life, was vital in telling my story in creating a new narrative based on truth. But to understand it, I had to realize why dot number 3 came before dot #290 and whether or not they are connected in a beneficial and productive way. I had to ask myself and answer my own questions to become the artist of my picture story.

For a long time, I couldn't hold a writing utensil to connect the dots, much less connect them. Alcohol, drugs, trauma and eventually low self-esteem, addictions' saddest and most detrimental outcome, blocked me from ever believing a beautiful picture existed, much less one in color.

Today, I tell my story and continue adding to its beautiful picture.

Today, my constructed spiritual mantra is: "I do not say no to anything that will help me not harm myself or others with my thoughts, words or actions, one day at a time." As early sobriety successfully moved forward, I put the work into establishing a strong spiritual foundation in my new life. As I spoke to my parents every morning and throughout the day in prayer or simple conversation, my decisions became clearer and more productive in outcome. With responsibility towards the present external world and combating my past, I copiously engaged in an internal reformation of my thoughts and emotional management. I needed to format these with selfish spiritual beliefs that would eventually blossom into a living mantra.

My rippling mantra, which I had constructed and with which I empowered myself, was my edifice that would either be honored or destroyed with my own decisions and new behaviors. It equally and mutually became my creation and responsibility.

My living mantra, stated above, empowers me to stop and think what tool or resource would benefit my decision and create the optimal outcome. Awareness is 85% prevention and if I can't prevent something negative from happening, it is my mission to minimize my losses in negative experiences.

My high school, Northeast Catholic, mantra is "Tenui Nec Dimittam" "I have taken hold and will not let go." This provides me the willingness to grasp, hold onto, solidify and live by my mantra's assets. It's the foundation to my wellness and how I relate to the world in sobriety.

One scenario in my life may have me relating to the teachings of Buddha, while another situation may benefit from remembering what my mother or father said growing up. The belief must come from within myself, so that the truth and the support in finding direction becomes available and applicable.

Some of my precious gems are contained in my path of addiction. The tools I found during my addiction are equally valuable as the lessons obtained through sobriety. Some days and decisions simply surround the notion that I don't want to be that man I was in active addiction. It motivates and strengthens me that the truth of who I was, does not reflect who I want to be or who I am today.

I make the deliberations and decisions cautiously and appropriately. I use toll booths as a metaphor of my spiritual decision making. Today, we have express lane EZpass lanes where cars speed through at 45 MPH. That's how I made decision in my addictions; fast with no qualitatively reflection or thought of consequences. In the single EZ pass lane a car slows down to about 20 miles per hour, not stopping, relying on technology to pay the tool. Those are the decisions I made in early recovery, as I was not fully spiritual in *Brillism* or comfortable in leaning on supports or role models. Today, my decision making model has a human being in the booth, where I fully stop and greet a person, pay my toll and go on my way forward. That toll person and the art of slowing down represent *Brillism and Simodelism*. I make my decisions in a slow and deliberate manner by tapping the examples and spiritual assets acquired over time. With further deliberation, I chose whether or not I need to do something or let the chips fall where they may.

Do we think our way into good behaviors or do we act/behave our way into good thoughts about ourselves? I do both, while not focusing on the supposed negative or positive outcomes. The process of decision making is crucial and deserves attention and caution. I do everything with raised consciousness into the why I'm doing something. My client thought 278 times about why he was walking by the front door in treatment. I think about myself in a positive light and it guides me towards better behavioral actions. The vital ingredients lie in awareness and consciousness of the whys I am doing something or feeling a certain way. What conscious action caused the positive or negative outcomes? Over time, more purpose and meaning developed in my life.

In early sobriety, people told me to stick around and wait for the miracle to happen. I spent months wondering what the fuck is the miracle. Can anyone tell me? Well allow me to pull back the wizard's curtain. Spoiler alert: The miracle of sobriety is that when all your past liabilities in life become your greatest assets in constructing a meaningful, productive and fruitful life. Self-esteem at its finest!

CHAPTER 17

I Don't Want To Die

It's 6/8/2018, while writing this book, I have established that 2018 has been my roughest year of life, especially in sobriety. Something else is wrong.

On New Year's Eve, I suffered through my first bout of the flu. It floored me for three days. On January 17th, after needing to cancel the operation due to flu, I had an umbilical hernia repair operation. March brought on my second flu battle. In mid-April, after having my first encounter with 48-hour constipation, I soon found myself in the hospital for three days, diagnosed with diverticulitis. My attempts at weight loss consuming many breakfast nut bars took a toll on my colon and lower abdomen. Over two weeks, I lost at least a pound a day and knew there was something wrong.

My original cat scan showed two enlarged lymph nodes on my upper abdominal area, which now has me nervous and scheduled for an appointment with an oncologist. They say to pay attention to the body, it truly is a temple. I am paying attention and again, something is wrong. My decreased appetite, continued weight loss, stress and depression has me pointing in one direction. I don't want to share this with anyone because I want to be wrong. The reality is that I don't know and I'm doing the responsible thing and following up with those that can know, my doctors. I take solace in my efforts and attempt, at all costs, to stray from predicting or hanging my hat on the unknown. Thank God for the Serenity Prayer.

I don't want to die. However, after 15 years of sobriety, I often feel that I've lived 100 lifetimes, engaging and embracing life's moments to the fullest. The good and bad times, through my education and lectures of the Yin and Yang, say these polar-opposites are relatable and connected. You cannot fully understand or embrace one without the other. My addiction has provided me with a perception of life, through sobriety, that I once could never fully appreciate.

After my neutral cat scan in mid-June, I was back in the hospital for 3 more days with my second bout of diverticulitis. Results of the neutral scan concluded that the lymph nodes were still present, even bigger. During my hospital stay, they biopsied the lymph nodes. After being discharged, I was permitted to embark on my vacation to Colorado. A majestic vacation in the state where everywhere is a picture. I visited friends, played golf and attended my first concert at Red Rocks. We embarked from Colorado following two great nights with Dead and Company at Folsom Field.

On my first day home, I followed up with my oncologist. On June 16, 2019, my greatest fears came true. I was diagnosed with at a tumor, *Paraganglioma*. The first thing out of my oncologist's mouth pertained to the lottery type statistics of the rarity of my tumor −2 out of one million people are diagnosed a year. This type of tumor secretes adrenaline causing strokes and heart attacks. It is frequently misdiagnosed or goes undetected. He added, "In 28 years of being an oncologist, I'd be lying if I said I ever saw this diagnosis and type of tumor."

After consultation, I was referred to my miracle doctor at Penn Medicine. In the first 5 minutes of our consultation, he asked me about golfing in Colorado. I was put at ease. Through his approachability, humaneness and professional development, I knew I was with the right doctor. His friendly rapport precluded his amazing medical knowledge and skills. Each ingredient of our conversation added to my security and wellness. While still nervous and sad, he secured his role as the preserver and healer of my life.

After blood tests, it was reconfirmed as Paraganglioma. As I sat at my desk in work one afternoon, after submitting my 24h-our urine test, I received a phone call from my doctor. He announced that he only received one of the blood tests back and immediately added in layman's terms, "We got to get that thing out of there." If norepinephrine (adrenaline) safe levels are 80-150, my level was just shy of 1,200. I don't know for how long, but this tumor was wreaking havoc and was most likely changing me in ways

I didn't fully realize or understand. I called and set a date in September for the extraction of the tumor. I made arraignments with work

On Saturday August 11th, I texted my brothers and work supervisor, informing them that I would be in the hospital later that day. I knew that my third bout of diverticulitis was upon me. It proved to be the worst case of the three. At 11pm, riddled with pain, I called my friend to come take me to the hospital. I couldn't drive.

I was admitted into Doylestown Hospital at 12:30am. By 4pm, that afternoon, I was transferred down to Penn Medicine. I never experienced so much pain. Reassured of my doctor choice, at 3:30am, Monday morning, my eyes squinted open. Standing over me, with concern and care, stood my doctor. Surprised, I struggled, asking, "what are you doing here?" He immediately stated, "I heard you were here buddy and I'm here for you." He immediately shared his collaboration with my new miracle doctor, a Penn Medicine Colon and Rectal Surgeon. He shared with me that my tumor is the number one priority. He insisted on the collaboration to get me well, so that the two doctors could perform a double surgery, removal of the tumor and colon resection.

After 6 days of sheer pain and an ongoing day to day call on whether I would be placed on the emergency operating table, I began feeling some relief. My team of doctors and their Plan A became a reality.

After 9 days, I was discharged from the hospital. I was placed on TPN, a port for nutritional intake. For six weeks, I hooked myself up to my "bag of dinner" for 12 hours a night. I consumed nothing by mouth for 5 weeks. Relieved, after 5 weeks, I was permitted to start a slow BRAT (bananas, rice, applesauce, toast) diet. My diet proceeded as a BAT (bananas, applesauce and toast), eliminating the rice ingredient. This treatment plan was engaged in order for my colon to heal and be prepared for the extraction of my sigmoid colon and resection to my rectum.

On September 10th, the double operation took place. My first ever operation, an outpatient umbilical repair, in my life occurred earlier this year. Now, less than 9 months later, I was having a major double surgery. I awoke to 21 staples down the center of my stomach and one of my worst realities coming true. In order for the colon to heal, I was fitted with an ileostomy bag. A portion of my intestine was pulled out and bagged to bypass my newly resected colon for its healing. It was unknown on whether or not it would be temporary or permanent. The next three months were staggeringly stressful and mind bending. It was traumatic.

Eventually, I had my post operation tumor follow up tests. The tests and pathology of the tumor came back negative. The tumor had a score of 3, signifying it being benign. It also revealed itself as a slow-moving tumor. I was relieved, even while still living with the ileostomy bag. It was a daunting chore to experience contradictory emotions, simultaneously. I received the positive news on the tumor, but still had a battle in front of me. I could never let myself "go there" in full gratitude. I tried, but often unsuccessfully. Gratitude is truly achieved.

After 3 months of living with an ileostomy bag, I received the jubilant news that it would be reversed. On December 12th, the reversal operation took place successfully. To say I was relieved, grateful and happy would be an understatement. Sometimes, words just can't cover the truest essence of raw emotions. My follow up appointment declared a return date to work. I was signed off by both my doctors, after 10 months of mind-boggling health issues.

Seven short months ago, I sat across from my brothers handing over my will, life insurance policies and financial account information. I was preparing for the worst-case scenario, as a responsible human being.

If I haven't already stated, this was and will always be trauma in my life. I will deal with this on a daily basis for the rest of my life. I will be reminded by yearly tests, scans and follow ups. I will live and eat cautiously, adopting a new wellness reality as my ongoing healing continues. My healing is not over. More importantly, I will live life through the lessons provided by my illness and the love and support of so many people, including my family, friends and medical team at Penn Medicine.

During my illness and recovery, I primarily lived with my brother Joe and his wife, Deb. My nieces and nephews: Erin, Drew, Christian, Elena and Dorothy from wherever they were living poured out love and support for their, Uncle Dude (I must be the cool Uncle, with a nickname like that). On some occasions, I relocated to the Lehigh Valley, to live with my brother Bob and his wife, Joyce. I am in tears right now, typing this paragraph, as they taught me what unconditional, altruistic, family love truly is. Their company, encouragement, support, love and support throughout my illness has been stoic and stellar, beyond human comprehension. Again, words sometimes diminish the reality. I do not think I could have done this without them. Their rides and presence at all of my appointments were concrete assets in remaining focused and motivated to partake in my healing. They created the fighter in me. I thank my family endlessly and I can only promise to live a sober and productive life to show my gratitude for their compassion and love. My spirituality and responsible commitment to their love kept me sober during this traumatic event.

Lastly, I would like to thank my employer, extended family and friends for their outpouring of love and support, during my health issues. The correlation between traumatic health issues and humane love revealed a light of positivity that will radiate in my soul forever. The Facebook messages, texts, calls, visits, cards and care packages sustained my human spirited ambition to create a personal quest in defeating my illness. The good always outweighs the bad. Your example of kindness reassures me this fact. Each day, I live to breathe another moment of life's cherished gifts, I carry each of you with me.

I wrote this book while sick with the energy each person provided me during my fear of death. The absolute truth in all of these pages is from your energy, while igniting my hope to inspire others. You all made this book possible and a reality.

Namaste – *I appreciate the light of my world better, now that your light has entered mine.*

CHAPTER 18

Santa Is Real

With the title of the book and front cover picture, I assume this is the chapter and subject matter for which you, the reader, have been patiently awaiting. My ongoing assumption, while creating this book, was that it may influence the positive potential of all readers. Most importantly, my intention was to give hope and possibly initiate change in treating addictions. I attempted to reach many audiences.

As the title of the book usually raises interest, suspicion and suspense, the subject of Santa Claus and the awesome experience of portraying such a legendary, ageless and indisputable figure encouraged me to open up and share my life story. I don't know whether it was playing Santa Claus, or being surrounded by families and children, during such a happy time of the year, that affected me the most. I'm sure it all contributed.

All of the subject matter of my story has been brewing and bubbling for a long time. I have been clean and sober for over 16 years and have had countless blessings and experiences that could have spawned such a book. During my addictions, overdoses, arrests, suicide attempts and homelessness did not bring me into treatment. It was an accumulation of negative consequences, bringing me to point of hopelessness, where a moment of spiritual clarity brought me to treatment. During recovery, employment, educational, travel, love, family and blessings did not spearhead my book. Taking up the role of Santa Claus, in December of 2017, created the culminating and qualifying experience in becoming my positive personal creation.

The original title of the book was the name of this chapter, *Santa Is Real*. However, I didn't want to become a spoiler of the miracle of Christmas to any children that might wander past the book in stores, or if it was on the coffee table in clear view for children to see. I didn't want the question of Santa's realness to surface in children before "it's time." As adults, we all know this cherished process. We each have our own stories of revelation. The eventual exposure is often a life development marker that is confusing and sometimes sad for both parent and child. It is one of the exiting realizations taking a child into another phase of their development. Moreover, a parent witnesses a child's innocence depleting. A child growing up, in all stages of development, is a delicate and unavoidable realization for all parents.

For the third time in my life, I was provided an amazing episode of primary experiential education of Santa Claus becoming a reality in my heart. The first was the beginning years of my childhood innocence; where I was provided this awesome universal belief in a kind, selfless and overworked iconic man, in a red suit, who worked one night a year for every home and family in the world. Everything that happens during the holiday season of Christmas reinforces this awesome belief.

The second time was later in life, 41 years old, when my girlfriend, eventual wife, provided me the opportunity to play Santa. There was no red suit or fluffy white beard. Together, we were in charge of reinforcing the miracle of Christmas for her beautiful daughters. It was a late-night sneaking around the house as my two (eventual) step daughters slept upstairs. I cut carrots, poured milk, carried and wrapped presents, built toys, stuffed stockings, tip toed cautiously and most of all, I cried like a baby. At moments, I needed to walk outside to hyperventilate and not wake the girls. It is at these gifted moments, I remembered I was a homeless alcoholic, living in a park, who never dreamed of such an occasion or opportunity. I did not feel worthy. This was not supposed to happen to me. I was supposed to die in my addictions. Needless to say, I didn't take this role lightly. I believed!

Ironically, the third time participating in this role of playing Santa Claus initiated the writing of this chapter and eventual book. This last chapter, I wrote first.

For the past 14 years, I have been performing acoustic guitar music and singing at a beautiful mall located in Bucks County, PA. Sometimes I perform solo and other times, most recently, with my friend. Our Americana/Bluegrass duo is named Spinning Straw. Other times, when solo, it is just Mike Brill. (www.mikebrill.com / www.spinningstraw.net)

Peddlers Village is an outdoor colonial style mall that attracts 2 million visitors a year. All of the stores are outdoors, unlike the huge modern malls; while being the furthest thing from a strip mall. Peddlers Village has stone pathways winding around a multitude of unique wooden storefronts. The pathways are highlighted with breathtaking foliage; becoming the centerpiece of tourists' and residents' photos. The center green area is highlighted by a huge gazebo on top of a hill. The gazebo is located in the forefront of an old barn; complete with a functional waterwheel.

During the holiday Christmas season, the village radiates over one million Christmas lights. The lights and decorations are revealed, for the first time, during the Grand Illumination Event, inaugurating the holiday shopping season.

Throughout the year, the village celebrates the holidays, seasons and natural farming area by giving attention to the seasonal gifts of fruits. Through Strawberry, Peach, Blueberry and Apple Festivals; while celebrating the holiday seasons through Spring, Summer, Fall and Winter festivals, I have had the privilege of adding a soundtrack to the ambiance and festivities. This beautiful and tranquil space in Bucks County, PA truly initiates, within each visitor, a meditative retail therapeutic alliance and process.

For the past 14 years, performing at Peddler's Village is truly a highlight of my yearly music schedule. Weather permitting, the festival shoppers become appreciators of the musical and artistic vibrations provided by the artists and musicians. My first performance at the village was spearheaded by my friend, the owner of my favorite store, The Celtic Rose Irish Shop. She initiated a village Celtic Festival and I was honored to be one of the Irish Music performers. That day of the Irish Festival, the village's Festivals Director, recruited me for their upcoming summer festival. I have been performing there ever since.

Brill performing at a Peddlers Village festival

In November 2017, after completing my two sets of music for the holiday kickoff parade, I discussed the upcoming schedule of the Christmas Festival. The present Festivals Director expressed his concern for the upcoming seasonal Santa Claus schedule. He organizes the traditional Visitation and Pictures with Santa. He declared he was lacking humans and struggling to fill the full schedule of worthy and willing men to take on the magical role of Santa Claus. I crossed the boundary, feeling comfortable with the Director and asked if he would allow me to help. He lit up and said "would you be able to help me? If so, that would be amazing!" He then instructed me of the menial financial pay for this position. In absolute and authentic shock, I responded, "It pays?.......this is on my bucket list." I was simply honored with the opportunity.

After my initial excitement subsided, our conversation steamed forward, exploring specific shifts. I became nervous and almost hesitant. Questions of worthiness flooded my head. In a heartbeat, I went from excited to feelings of inadequacy. Inside my diabolical mind, I started creating excuses to get out of my role and responsibility. Can Santa call out sick? The alcoholic mind and old behaviors flooded my consciousness. I ended the conversation abruptly with a true and consistent addict response, that came in the form of a selective excuse or a "side door" to escape the responsibility. I told him that I would check my availability and email him dates and times.

That night, I went home and sat alone, in my apartment, wondering why, after 14 years of performing at the village, the opportunity of playing Santa Claus, occurred 2 months after my devastating separation from my wife and family. Rather than crying again that night, I seized the moment and emailed the Director my available dates and times to play Santa.

The blessings of opportunity defeated the burdens of the past; because I let it.

For the past 27 years, I have stood on a stage, behind a microphone, strumming a guitar and performing music in front of thousands of people, performing approximately 5,000 shows. It has been the absolute one consistent and positive healing aspect of my life. It became most prevalent in my sober years. It stands as my therapy and a huge ingredient to my wellness. Although music was wrongfully motivated and perceived, through an egotistical approach, during the most difficult times in my life, music has transformed the substance of my connections to people and life. Music performance is a living and breathing organism. It is an extension of my being. It thrives to fight for survival, consistently providing a passage back to my personal balance and serenity. It is the high that I've searched for, for so many years.

Before every musical performance, I find myself in a complex state of nervousness. I become fidgety and disoriented. No matter how many times I've performed, this is my reality before performing. The first rule of processing emotions, especially nervousness, is giving yourself the permission to feel. I struggle through my first song. By the end of that song, I am in my glory.

Living is feeling.

An hour before my first shift as Santa, I arrived at the village. I met with the Director and was introduced to Santa's gear. A beautiful red velvet jacket and pants, knee-high black leather boots, a curled white mustache and combed wig, a big black belt and a red hat with a fluffy white ball at the end, hung in the preparation office. Immediately, I embraced my beloved high school, North Catholic Falcon's colors. The same colors, red and white, embracing me in similar yet different meanings. I was connecting the dots. As Santa Claus and a North Catholic Falcon, the mission is the same. I am preserving on ongoing tradition of pride and human development.

As I stood by the legendary Santa suit, I began to imagine the vast stories and interactions I would have with the children and families. The Director redirected me from my vivid imagination and instructed me to sit down. It was make-up time. The ideal image of a "good" Santa Claus is a natural look. I neither had the weight or white facial hair to pull of that reality. The Director had the tools and skills to create a parallel to this beloved image. With professional touches, he glued the mustache and eyebrows on my face, adding a slight touch of rouge, creating the rosy cheeks of Santa's smile. The wig, that sat preserved on a mannequin's head, was brushed delicately and then placed on my head. He combed the wig repeatedly, stepping back numerous times, to perfect the look. He reached for the jacket, and I questioned him where the pillow was, to add weight to my 185-pound frame. The Director, in his years of Santa preparation experience, instructed me that the fake weight is unnatural. The size of the suit and the way I sit on the chair would represent a naturally fuller Santa.

As he was putting the jacket on me, completing the preparations, I belted out a "Ho, Ho, Ho" in my greatest baritone voice. Immediately, he denounced my vocal efforts. He further instructed that a fake Santa voice scares child, more than preserving their belief. Everything the Director did and instructed me to do, was to create the perfect picture moment. He produced every trick of the trade, to improve the chances of getting the children comfortable and smiling for their picture with Santa. His enthusiasm for this desired reality swept through me. I felt prepared, while being nervous.

Fully dressed as Santa Claus, he took a few pictures and we prepared to walk through Giggleberry, the location where the Visitation and Pictures with Santa takes place. Giggleberry, at Peddlers Village, contains an old authentic sized carousel, interactive foam ball room, video games and snack bar restaurant. The video games produce winning tickets for simply participating in the games. The mini store is always busy with children and parents cashing in their winning tickets for a prized memory of their day at the village. It is the perfect setting for the Christmas Miracle.

As I strolled towards Santa's throne, I was immediately thrusted into the cherished role. Families smiling and children swarming, impeding Santa's steps. I waved to families and hugged children. Some children ran away. The spirit and mystery were mutually alive. The line of awaiting and anxious children, with their parents, was long. Their goal of the perfect Santa picture was soon to become a reality. I sat down on the assigned Santa seat and the Director, again in his professionalism, had the camera take a few solo shots. They were checking the lighting, shadows and of course, the authentic perception of me, Santa Claus. I turned to the crowds of people and produced my best parade wave and smiled to excite the children. I'm not sure who was more excited, the children or their beloved Santa Claus. I looked back at the entrance.

I rarely sat dormant, as the visitors just kept coming. I witnessed and reinforced the Christmas miracle for all. I felt the spirit come over me, through the children. The dialogue of wishes, love, kindness and believing, provided by the children, were overwhelming. As my emotions became authenticated, I looked up at the next family in line.

A mother and father approached Santa holding two new born infants. Santa's greatest challenge were infants. The team of professional elves promoted tips and efforts in safety and security of the babies. The parents approached and greeted Santa Claus. They informed Santa that the infants were 5 months old. A beautiful reality swept through my Santa suite and directly infiltrated my mind and heart. I was to be in the picture with twin babies on their first Christmas. Furthermore, this picture, for many years, would be a permanent Christmas decoration in this family's home. In 18 years, as the twins went off to college and with the parent's missing their babies, I can almost guarantee, this Santa picture would find a new, more visible location in their home, commemorating childhood and their first Christmas.

Now, I completely understood the Director's mission and commitment. This was no ordinary picture, this was an investment in preserving family values and memories. I sat in Santa's skin wondering if the family should know I was a homeless alcoholic. I looked at the entrance.

As the carousel went in circles with lights flashing and Christmas music blaring, I cherished the here and now with each child. I watched scared and crying children light up with happiness, after becoming comfortable with Santa. I held squirming, yelling kids, whose parents unconditional love and contentment surfaced, after revealing a not-so-perfect picture. They laughed and will laugh again for many years of this imperfect memory with Santa. While the pictures were initially important to these parents, they vividly displayed the meaning of Christmas through their acceptance. Being together is all that mattered.

On one visitation I held a brother, 10 years old; and a sister, 8 years old. Their parents stood by smiling, as the children independently and courageously took a seat on Santa's lap. I immediately saw a look of sheer concern on the young girl's face. I assumed there was anxiety in seeing Santa up close and personal. I addressed the young girl first. She waved me down closer. She lifted her hand to her mouth to share a secret wish list and I turned my ear to her mouth. She whispered in Santa's ear that this morning she broke her big brother's electronic toy. She told Santa that she wanted nothing for Christmas, except for Santa to replace her brother's toy, that she broke. Eight years old and she wanted nothing, but to make up for what she did and make her brother happy. Santa began crying and turned to the young boy. At 10 years old, he stated that he wanted nothing for Christmas. He simply wanted to be surrounded by his family and that is what he is most looking forward to during the holidays. Children teaching Santa.

As we took the pictures and the parents collected the children, they approached the digital screen, as a family, to choose and purchase their memorable picture package. This visit could not end. Santa, filled with the true meaning of Christmas, taught to him by 8 and 10-year-old siblings, asked his elf to bring the father back. These parents were not walking away without knowing the affect their children had on Santa. The father approached me and with tears in Santa's eyes, I thanked the father and commended he and his wife's job in raising two wonderful kids. I told him about his children's requests and let him know that his children taught Santa about life and the selfless acts that are necessary to live a fruitful life.

As the next children sat on my lap, I looked up and saw the previous parents with pictures in hand and arms around their children. The father looked over at Santa and with tears coming down his face, he mouthed the words clearly "Thank You." I smiled, waved and looked over at the entrance doorway.

The challenges were not challenging that day. They became a part of the story. Children will be children; while parents will be parents. I witnessed personalities and traits that were not mine. I embraced each one. I realized the holidays don't mean the same to everyone. Everyone has their story. No matter what, the Visitation to Santa brings forth a moment of embracing while letting go. No matter the religion or culture, a child's belief and the miracle of Christmas, celebrated and cherished all over the world, is somehow manifested and nurtured in each person.

Over the course of three shifts, I held at least 30 children for their first Christmas. First Christmases and teenage rebellion, in sitting on Santa's lap, were realities equally embraced by parents. This Santa is a counselor and I witnessed the chapters of my Human Development textbook come to life. We all have stages of life. In those stages, we have roles, expectations and achievements. No one goes through life the same way. Life doesn't come with a cookie cutter. Parents and children are the circle of life. Generational confirmation brings forth the ingredients of identity and tradition. We are family. A family of humans, spinning on this blue ball, around the sun. There is a responsibility to ourselves and to each other. The responsibility is preservation of life; through kindness. We, as humans, need to give ourselves a break and incorporate the holiday spirit into our lives, more than just once a year. I looked over at the entrance.

My third shift, as Santa, was a long 8 hours, with a lunch break. I did not eat cookies and milk. I had a cheesesteak, like any good respectable Philadelphian. The Christmas spirit had not worn out, within me. Rather, it was emotionally draining. I experienced every emotion through my own, children's and parents'. I embraced the positivity. At one point, the photographer stated to me, that while they appreciate the twinkle in my eye, the tears were a bit much. I am Irish and wear my heart on my sleeve. Even if it is Santa's sleeve.

I looked over at the entrance.

As my final shift was coming to an end, I realized the entire time I was partaking in one ongoing and consistent movement. It struck me that the visitation line was to my right and the entrance to Giggleberry was to my left. This parameter encased me. As I was focusing on children and the holiday miracle for others, I was subconsciously denying my own reality of emotional processing.

I realized my tenure as Santa Claus was coming to an end. For me, it became a sad end. It crippled me. I needed to breath and asked for a drink of water. They paused the line and staff inquired if I needed a break. Everyone wondered if Santa was alright. I was having a panic attack, fueled by a raw emotion. I realized that after 22 hours of playing Santa Claus and preserving this ageless miracle of faith and happiness, in all people, I was missing my own ingredients of life. After each visit to Santa, for 22 hours, I was swiveling my head towards the entrance hoping and praying. Santa's only item on his Christmas list, was hoping his wife and two step daughters would walk in to visit me, their Santa Claus. For the first time in 6 years, I would not be Santa Claus at home.

For a year, I told people my story of portraying Santa Claus. I shared the beautiful honor, while always ending the story in dramatic fashion, with my own sad tale and reality of missing my family.

After the following Christmas of 2018, during my sickness, I met with a friend. My friend and author, Tom Schied, met me to discuss the writing and publication of my book. Tom wrote a heartwarming book, *The Mustard Jar*, a story of family, friends and music set in Northeast Philadelphia, during the 1980's. Tom listened with great attention to my book ideas and tale of playing Santa Claus. I shared Santa's emotional parameters. I finalized my story with the usual reality of missing my family. He humbly brought me down to another reality. Tom asked me, "You know why your family didn't show up?" I murmured some excuses or ideas of speculation. He simply said, like only a true friend could say, "It (playing Santa Claus) wasn't about you, Mike." He went on to explain that I was provided an awesome blessing of partaking in so many others' Christmas celebrations. It was about them, all the children who would find joy in Santa. It was about preserving the miracle of the season. What was missing in my life, is what I wanted to focus on. What was missing, was provided in another way. After 14 years of providing music for the village, I got asked to be Santa Claus, 2 months into my separation. Now, there's a bigger picture of energy to look at and embrace.

After my final shift, while alone in the changing room office, I slowly disrobed from being Santa Claus. I cried. I prayed. I bargained. I hoped. I dreamed. I wondered. My role was over; but the new reality and responsibility of moving on in my life; with a daily, never-ending mission of sustaining the Christmas spirit, consumed me. In my hoodie, sweatpants and backpack, I hung up Santa's jacket, put the wig back on the mannequin and exited the office. Wiping tears from my eyes, my sneakers took 12 steps down the hallway. I approached children and families. Without hesitation, I began smiling and waving, just like Santa Claus. I got some bewildered looks of confusion from parents. Children ignored me. People hesitantly waved back, wondering who I was and what I was doing.

In an instant, I forgot, I was not in the Santa suit anymore. I was back to being Mike Brill. I stopped waving but continued smiling at every person. I lifted my head; put my shoulders back and happily walked through the crowds of people.

Today, I am someone. I know who I am. I am a survivor. I am in recovery. I am proud of myself. Today, I enjoy being me. I can't wait for what is next to come on my journey.

Hello, my name is Mike Brill, who played Santa, and I'm a grateful recovering alcoholic.

Printed in the United States
By Bookmasters